JailLyfe

"JailLyfe": Jesus Is Always Looking

Love Your Friends & Your Enemies

JailLyfe: Jesus Always Is Looking
Love Your Friends & Your Enemies

Special Thanks

There are many people in my life who have been extremely influential. First and foremost, I would like to thank God Almighty for His constant watch, care and protection over my life. I would like to thank my parents, Vonzell (Deceased) and Gwen Chancy. Throughout all of my foolishness they have stood with me helping me in many areas that I struggle with on a day-to-day basis. I love you guys and am grateful to have you all as my parents, and look forward to seeing my father again in Heaven.

I would also like to say a special thank you to my brother, Adam Chancy, who has been on this journey with me throughout my entire life, through the ups and downs. I love you, and proud to call you, my brother. To each of my children (Xavier, Shynik, Nehemiah, Aaron II aka Tato, the twins Summer & Simone, Andrew, Zemora and Caysen) I would like to say that I love you guys and I'm proud of each and every one of you and hope that you don't just see the failures of my life, but see the things that I've fought to overcome and be the best father to you guys as possible.

To my extended family, aunts, uncles and cousins, I want to say thank you for all of your prayers and love throughout my life, I love you guys.

To my friends that I have gained and lost throughout the years, I love you guys and am thankful to have shared a portion of my life with you and happy that you have been able to share a portion of my life with me.

To my close friends, Byron Green, Michael Hylton and others, some that I can mention and others that I cannot, thank you guys for being true friends!

Additionally, a very special thanks to Kathleen Hill, Brandon Bernard (Deceased), Prescott Smith, as evidenced in chapter 18. Love all of you guys!

Last, but definitely not least, to my wife Shackarah Chancy, you are amazing, beautiful, supportive and the love of my life. Thank you for your constant belief in me, your friendship and your love on our countdown to forever. I love you.

Table of Contents

Chapter 1: The Beginning of the End

Chapter 2: Early Years

Chapter 3: Lost: Who Am I?

Chapter 4: Every Young Black Male's Aspirations: Basketball & Football

Chapter 5: The Music Got Me

Chapter 6: The House Party

Chapter 7: Juvenile Detention Center

Chapter 8: Jail

Chapter 9: Hangin' with the Gangsta's

Chapter 10: Charged as an Adult

Chapter 11: Prison Boot Camp

Chapter 12: Freedom, but Still Breaking the Law

Chapter 13: Penitentiary Bound

Chapter 14: The Bank Robbery

Chapter 15: Moving Marijuana Through U.P.S.

Chapter 16: Girls, Girls, Girls

Chapter 17: (That) Beginning of the End

Chapter 18: Everybody Doesn't Make It Back

Chapter 19: Past, Present & Future

Chapter 20: Pictures of the Past & Present

Terminology Defined

Chapter 1:

OD-Overdose

Uppers-Drugs that are Stimulants

Cocaine Spook-A Paranoid Feeling

Coke-Powdered Cocaine

Ex-Pills-Ecstasy, which is a Drug

Homeboys-Friends

Blunt-Weed (Marijuana) Rolled in Cigar Wraps that have been Emptied of the Tobacco

Chapter One

"The Beginning of the End"

During the last six months of my running from God, I immersed myself heavily in drug usage, attempting to O.D. while tryin' to "fry" the Holy Spirit out of my mind! Tired and frustrated, I wanted to be done with life and finished with hearing God's voice trying to get my attention. Although I had a .38 caliber pistol, I had no interest in taking the messy way out by shooting myself in the head. So, what better way than to consume so many drugs at one time that I would simply die in my sleep never again to wake up from the high?

But I'm getting ahead of myself; here's the beginning of the end:

On **Sunday, April 6th, 2008**, in the city of B.R., short for Baton Rouge, Louisiana, I began my day as I normally liked, a little breakfast to hold the alcohol. Then it was time to begin my intoxicants. Starting with beer, I downed thirteen 12-ounce cans of *Bud Light*, then I snorted a $20 bag of Cocaine that I had gotten from the rapper Lil' Boosie's neighborhood on BR's South Side, while also smoking some weed with a co-worker of mine. How was I able to function throughout the day? Simple answer: I had built up such a high tolerance for drugs and alcohol from steadily taking them since I was 15 that at

25, though I had a small frame and only weighed 150 pounds, I could "handle my alcohol", as the saying goes.

Monday, April 7th, 2008, was no exception. You see, I wasn't just a weekend drug user; this was an everyday event, a seven-days-a-week habit that I was driven to fulfill.

That day I had enough money to buy a double-stack Ecstasy pill that I popped, but I later found it was mixed with too much "speed," which caused me not to sleep properly for the next two days. Through it all, I didn't see that God was silently at work, ordering events in my life in several ways.

Wednesday, April 9th, 2008,

rolled around. It was the day that was to forever change my life. Like other days, this day was no exception to my rule. I snorted a dime bag of Cocaine, although I knew the chemicals from the powder constantly corroded my nostrils, causing frequent nosebleeds. Yeah, I knew that the things I was doin' had harmful effects on me, but at the time I did all these drugs my only thought was relief from reality and the fun of being high, which drowned out all thoughts of the drugs' negative effects.

As the day continued, I drank a 24-ounce can of *Bud Light* beer and smoked some weed with my next-door neighbor, while at the same time standing outside playin' around with a .22 Caliber rifle. Interestingly, the high from Monday's Ecstasy pill had not completely worn off; it was still in my bloodstream and affected my mind and body, keeping me from being able to sleep for the last few days.

I hadn't slept since Sunday night, which was normal because of the large amount of drug "uppers" that I consumed.

On the brink of self-destruction that Wednesday, I came inside the house at 11:30pm feelin' good from the high and doin' what I do! After coming into the house, I then went into my room, never to come out the same person again! As I was walking into the room, I stopped and stood in the doorway for a few seconds because I could immediately sense that there was an evil presence in the room! As I continued to go further into the room, a fear came upon me like never before! This was nothing like any Cocaine "spook" that I had experienced before. I could literally feel that something evil was in the room. After I closed the blinds, partly because of paranoia from the effects of the Marijuana and Cocaine, I laid down, "high as a kite," on my mattress and looked up at the ceiling. Boy, was I not ready to see what was happening there! My eyes seemed to be "opened" at that point, and I actually saw demons floating around on the ceiling wall. It was something like out of *Indiana Jones and the Raiders of the Lost Ark*, when at the end of the movie the "Ark of the Covenant" had been opened and demons began to weave in and out of people. It was a scary sight to behold, one that I will never forget!

What was happening in that room that night, I did not want to see! Like a little child I took the cover and pulled it over my eyes. The spiritual world seemed to be revealing itself to me, that veil that separates humanity and the spiritual realm was being pulled back. At that point I heard a voice, just as audible as someone speaking to me, but it was the voice of the

Holy Spirit, and he said something that I will never forget, calling me by name!

As clear as day, the Holy Spirit said, *"Aaron, either you get your life together now, or that's it!"*

Those very words frightened me to the very core of my bones! Why? Because I knew what the unpardonable sin was. I had grown up in the church and had a good understanding of what was going on at that point; I knew that the frightening words *"Let him alone, Ephraim is joined to his idols"* was about to happen to me. I was on the brink of committing the unpardonable sin, the only sin that God cannot forgive!

You see, for years I had been running from the Lord, and for the last 6-months, as I stated earlier, I was on a mission to "fry" the Holy Spirit out of my conscience. Every time I would hear the Holy Spirit trying to get my attention, I would purposely get "high" on coke, weed, Ex-Pills, prescription pills, alcohol, or possibly some Heroin, so that I could tune Him out. What in the world was I doing? On that fateful Wednesday, I realized just how much I had placed myself on dangerous ground, with Satan about to be allowed to have full control over my life!

After the Holy Spirit spoke to me, I knew that I had to do something. I was tryin' to think of whom I could call. I thought of my ex-wife, but I knew that she didn't want to hear anything from me, especially since our divorce papers had just come through. If I would have called any of my homeboys, they would have given me the common prescription that most friends that drink and do drugs would have said: "Drink a beer, smoke a blunt, go to sleep, then call me in the morning. Doctor's orders!" I knew I didn't need to hear that, so the only other person that I could think of calling was my dad. At the time he was in Georgia while I was in Baton Rouge, Louisiana, which meant there was an hour's difference between us. So, it was almost

1am where he was, and I knew that he would be asleep, but I had to throw out a lifeline to someone, hoping it would be grabbed, because I was on the verge of eternal destruction. I grabbed my cell phone and texted these very words, "*I feel lost and friendless.*"

After I sent the text message, I had no clue what was gonna happen next. After about five minutes my phone lit up with a response from my father. It stated these very words, *"What a friend we have in Jesus.*" Boy, was I happy to get that text! Immediately, I got on the phone and called my dad. We talked for about ten to fifteen minutes, and I poured my heart out to him, asking, "How can you and

Mom be so content with having no money, yet do full-time ministry work? And why am I so miserable—through all of the things that I had done in life, yet still no real joy?"

Before we finished talking, my dad stated that he would come out to Baton Rouge that coming Friday and pick me up. He advised me not to go to work the next day, where I was employed at a lube shop changing oil on cars, because he said that Satan would make sure that I forgot all about what happened the previous night. So, I made the decision that I would not go to work, instead, I would wait for him to come get me.

After talking, we prayed together.

Right after that, I got on my knees once again and began to pray for myself. It's always good for someone to be praying for you. No doubt you've heard of people saying that they would not be around "if it wasn't for a praying grandmother." Well, for me it was praying parents, but even though someone prays for you, you still at some point need to pray for yourself. That's what I did that night.

As I was on my knees praying to God, I could literally feel Satan and the weight of the world, in Jesus' name, rising off my back. This was a great feeling! One that everyone who's running from God can also experience! After I finished praying, I grabbed the Christian book, *The Great Controversy*, which so happened to be in my possession, and turned to chapter 32, "Snares of Satan". I knew that the devil was about to be on the prowl, and I had to begin reading to understand some of his tactics and filling my mind with spiritual things.

The next day, completely in a daze from the previous night's events, I continued reading Christian books like *Steps to Christ* and *Patriarchs and Prophets.*

My dad arrived in BR to pick me up by mid-Friday morning, having begun my journey to the Cross just hours earlier. I'm not gonna lie and say it was easy, because it wasn't by any means. For two months, I battled to overcome the drugs, alcohol, and nicotine addictions that I had, but one thing was for sure: I was determined to get on track! As I continued to come to the Cross, I read the Word of God (Bible) every morning, one chapter at a time, no matter what I would do during the day. As I continued doing this, I began to see that the Lord was cleaning me up. I came as I was, and I was allowing Jesus to change me instead of trying to change myself then coming to Jesus.

By **June 8th, 2008** God had taken all of those tastes away from me and now as you read this book, it has been over 15 years since I have used any drugs or drank any alcohol!

You reading this may be headed to the point of no return like I was. Or maybe you're on the run from God and are using many different drugs as I was doin', trying to kill yourself and/or trying to "fry" the Holy Spirit out of your mind.

Unconsciously, you may be inviting this same evil "presence" into your room and into your life as I was doing. Or maybe you are a loved one praying continuously for someone near and dear to you to return to God.

Continue to read this book! In it, you will find out more about my journey from the church to the streets and back to the fold of a loving God.

I experienced the life of *"The Prodigal Son"* described in Luke 15:11-32. You may find that some of my stories and experiences are relevant to the very thing(s) you go through on a day-to-day basis. And you may also find Jesus as you read on. But no pressure!

Now let's learn about my early years and see what led me to this point. For that we begin on October 3rd, 1982.

Terminology Defined

Chapter 2:

STD's=Sexually Transmitted Diseases

Pathfinder's-Similar to Boy scouts

Chapter Two

"Early Years"

Life for every individual began somewhere, sometime, and some day. For me, it was the Autumn of 1982 in Southwestern Michigan in a little town called Berrien Springs.

I really don't remember much about Berrien Springs as a young boy because after I was born, we didn't live there longer than several months. It wasn't until I was 16 years old (1999-2000) that I found myself back in Berrien Springs living there for a year, which will be talked about in a later chapter.

My mother, Gwen, and father, Vonzell, had two children. I am the youngest, as my brother Adam is two years older than I. Growing up, my brother and I had a very close relationship, but for many siblings, with growth comes changes, and for my brother and me, the changes also came as we grew.

I gravitated to the "darker" side of life, while he gravitated to success in school and careers, the "brighter side of life". Even though the bond grew weak, our brotherly love always remained, but it was hard to see for both of us at times.

More often than not, when you choose a certain type of lifestyle, not only are you going to be affected by what may happen to you while you're "out there", but your loved ones and anyone close to you are affected also.

If you do not believe me, ask the mothers, fathers, guardians and friends who have lost a child to gang violence; to life imprisonment behind bars; to STDs because of having unprotected sex; to drug overdose from trying to escape the reality of life; or to suicide because the child felt that there was no point to living.

Ask the mothers and the fathers who have to come to the jailhouse and prisons to visit their children, but can only "touch" them through the separating glass. See the tears that are shed as you're walking away from them into a life that is glorified by your favorite actor, musician or somebody you look up to that you knew wasn't living right.

Understand the amount of sleep that is lost because prayer is going up for you day and night while you're living estranged from family and seeking the "pleasures of sin," which only last for a short time.

With you, the family feels the pain that you go through, and it was no exception with my family. For years they wondered, "Where did we go wrong?"

I grew up in a household that would go to church on Saturday mornings, have family worship on Friday nights together, attend Pathfinders on Sunday's, and take part in Prayer Meetings on Wednesday nights. I went to a mixture of public and private schools. My parents firmly believed the text, which says, "Train up a child in the way that he should go…" I grew up knowing about the importance of the Bible to daily life, yet in still, none of it was enough to keep me from gravitating to the streets.

Most young people that gravitate to the lifestyle that I went to tend to have grown up in a single-parent home, live in a low-income area, have a parent or parents who are strung-out on drugs and seem as if they have nothing good going for them—all of which is a complete dichotomy to my upbringing.

So, what could have possibly led me to years of promiscuity, of drinking, smokin' weed, snortin' coke, using other drugs, and having a five-year prison sentence?

What led me, like the prodigal son in the Bible, to see what the world had to offer?

Did my parents go wrong, or did I go wrong? What happened?

Terminology Defined

Chapter 3:

Knock-Look Down on in a Condescending Manner

GD's-Gangster Disciples/Growth & Development

JailLyfe: Jesus Always Is Looking
Love Your Friends & Your Enemies

Chapter Three

"Lost: Who Am I?"

At some point in your existence, you may ask yourself, "Why am I here?" "What is my purpose in life?" "Who am I?" For years I pondered these same important questions that you may even now being asking yourself.

It wasn't until 2008, when I was 25, that I began to understand the answer to each of these challenging questions.

Somewhere along the way, I had lost my identity and could not figure out "who" I was. Sure, I knew my name was Aaron Chancy, but the question is deeper than just being able to recite what your name is, unfortunately, for years, I didn't know that!

I was lost, trying to figure out who I was by fitting in somewhere with some group of people.

While I was growing up in the 1980's my parents, being born and raised in West Philadelphia, did not have a lot of money, but they did have several things which I appreciate to this day and faithfulness to family is one of those things.

Once my dad told me that despite whatever circumstances may assail us, he did not want our family to become another statistical household, meaning that the father deserts the home when the child/children are young, leaving the mother to raise their child or children by herself. This was one of his personal principles.

The second thing that I appreciate about my parents is their determination to provide a good life for their family amid the hardships of life. Though it can be a challenge, and was a challenge for my parents, I saw the determination they had to keep climbing the proverbial ladder of societal success.

As a result of being poor, they both decided to go into the military. This provided us with monetary necessities and better housing, yet was still not a cure all for me personally; along the way I still found myself lost in situations that I quite possibly shouldn't have been lost in.

Military life can be a great experience, but at the same time it can be very difficult for some children, as it became in my case. People may say, "How could military life be a difficult experience for you, especially since you got the opportunity to live in Germany and Hawaii and see things that many young African-Americans may never see in life?" The answer to that is simple. What started out as being fun and new became a curse to me, because through them, I lost my identity.

This led to me losing my understanding of life's purpose, as well as the reason for my existence. Sure, living in foreign places can be fun-filled, but when you live in one place for three years and establish strong bonds and friendships with people, only to have them uprooted by the military's moving you far away to another state or another part of the planet, can be very disturbing to say the least. This only gets worse when, after staying in your new location for another three years, you are again uprooted—and the cycle continues.

I could never keep one set of friends like most people do. I never could get really close to a person because in a few years the friendship would be split apart by my family being uprooted to move somewhere else. In all the tangle of moving and settling, one mixes and mingles with people from all walks of life and nationalities, and at some point, you may lose who you are, as I did.

The loss of who I was, coupled with some other factors that will be discussed later, led me to a life that my parents never dreamed I would have gravitated towards. Looking back, I honestly would have rather stayed poor and in one location then having "a little more" and moving around constantly. It caused me to have attachment and detachment issues to say the least.

Just as many people in the streets find safety and love by being involved in a street gang like the "Bloods", "Crips", GD's, "Vice Lords", "Latin Kings", Mexican Mafia, or many other gangs, I to began to find that same comfort and friendship with those that society classifies as the "Thugs", "Outlaws", "Hustla's", and "Outcasts" of society. I was lost; I had lost my way, lost my purpose, lost hope, and lost my dreams.

By being lost, the devil found me, which is no place to be, and not who you want to be found by!

Terminology Defined

Chapter 4:

Hood-Generally a Low-Income

Neighborhood

And 1 Mixtapes-Collaboration of Multiple

Players that Play Street Basketball which,

Focuses on Fancy Moves and Plays

Seventh-day Adventist-Christian

Denomination

Sabbath-Saturday

Elder-A Church Leader

Sagging-Wearing Pants Below the Waist

Lids-Store Name that Sells Sports Teams

Items

Chapter Four

"Every Young Black Male's Aspirations: Basketball and Football"

My dad used to always say, "Find a job that you enjoy doing, so that when you do go to work, it's more like fun instead of a dreadful job."

"Finding something that I enjoy...." Hmmm.

Sports for many young black men and women are a way out of the 'hood', an escape from poverty, and a better option than a life of crime. It provides hope to many that are hopeless and monetary security to those who may or may not have had much in life. While my family wasn't suffering from poverty in every sense of the word because my parents had decided to go into the military to combat their lack of finances, I, nevertheless, had the same dreams of success in the sports world, specifically basketball and football.

I remember looking at my favorite NBA team back in the mid to late 1990's, the Chicago Bulls, primarily because of Michael Jordan, Scottie Pippen, and Dennis Rodman, who came a bit later, and just knew that sports was what I desired to do.

Learning Jordan's story of being cut from his High School basketball team, but the resilience to get on the team, get better and overall to win, was beyond amazing to me, and I wanted that!

In fact, there's a game that sticks in my mind like nothing else. For those who are too young to remember it, check it out online.

The game was the fifth one of the 1997 NBA Finals, it was the Bulls, with Michael Jordan and Scottie Pippen, against the infamous Utah Jazz, with Karl Malone and John Stockton. At this time, the Bulls' coach was Phil Jackson. In the game, Michael Jordan suffered severely from flu symptoms. In fact, the game is known in basketball history as the "Flu Game." Sick as Jordan was, he still played, because this was a crucial game in the series; a victory for either team would break their 2-2 tie at this point. Despite how he was feeling, Jordan played exceptionally well, showing much determination, motivation, and perseverance to help the Bulls win even against the Jazz's determined efforts.

With the series tied 2-2, game number five, Jordan sick with the Flu, but still playing, he ends up scoring 38 points to help the Bulls secure a win, 90 to 88, placing them 3-2 over the Utah Jazz in the series; one step nearer to their eventual championship.

Watching games like this one ignited me with passion for the game of basketball. Moreover, watching “And 1” Mix tapes with people like Hot Sauce, Skip 2 my Lou, and ½ Man ½ Amazing definitely solidified my dreams of professional basketball or maybe the “And 1” status, which was more street style basketball.

Playing NFL football was also a big dream of mine, even though most of my life I haven’t been big or muscular.

My favorite team was/is the Philadelphia Eagles, “Fly Eagles Fly.” I remember watching football games and seeing the great catches, the great hits, the great throws and wanting so badly to be a part of the NFL. If basketball didn’t work, I figured, maybe football would, or vice versa. I loved to watch guys like Randall Cunningham, Deion Sanders, Jerry Rice, and Barry Sanders, numerous greats in the league. Everyone that knows me, knows my love and passion for football and the Philadelphia Eagles!

"Sports Dreams Crushed"

Despite me having a strong passion to play sports, there were hindrances in my path to pro success. Those things which I saw as hindrances, which many people also may see as hindrances to "success" or to "fun", was the fact that I was a Seventh-day Adventist (SDA) Christian!

For some reading this that may not mean anything, but for those that understand what I mean, can relate very well.

This meant that I could not play any athletic games on Friday nights or Saturdays, of which most of the games that would be played for a rec center or for a public school happened during those times. Also, I went to several SDA Church schools, which did not promote playing sports on Saturdays.

By the time I was back in public high school, enabling me to play on Fridays and Saturdays, my dreams were crushed; I was smoking weed, smoking

Black & Mild's and drinking alcohol, all of which did not help my athletic skills.

God desires the service and allegiance of LOVE, but at that point I did not love God. Though I knew of Him from church and family devotions, I still did not have my own LOVE relationship with Him.

So, when I was told I couldn't play because of all these "SDA reasons," I thought to myself, "I hate church, God, and anything that has something to do with hindering this success that I badly want!" I'm sure many people can relate to this feeling!

Many of us as young people suffer from these same things. We desire to be great in this world, according to worldly standards, but because we have not developed a one-on-one love relationship with God, the "You cannot do" because of being a Seventh-day Adventist makes no sense and builds up a frustration within most of us.

I remember when I was 11-years old a local church elder asked me, "What are you going to do about the Sabbath if you play professional sports?" Although I didn't say it, in the back of my mind, I was thinking, "Who cares about the Sabbath! I want to play basketball or football." They were my goals! And questions like the Elder's frustrated me instead of making me think, but I was 11 years old, how much thinking was I really going to do?

It may not be a surprise to you reading this book, but I didn't make it to professional sports. As a matter of fact, I didn't graduate high school, play much sports during my short tenure there, nor seek any other type of career, but I was headed headfirst to a life of crime, drugs, alcohol and through the judicial system.

With my dreams crushed due to the lack of a LOVE relationship with God, the loss of my identity and forced religious rules; life for me was about to take a drastic turn and most of the morals that were instilled in me were on their way right out the window. It was time to start sagging my pants, turn the "Lids" fitted in another direction, get my ears pierced, delve heavily into the hip-hop culture, and skip school on a regular basis, since I wasn't paying attention anyhow.

No point in "wasting time being there!"

Terminology Defined

Chapter 5:

The Game-What we call street hustlin'

Hot Boi-Someone Who's Always in the Middle of Things that are Negative

Chapter Five

"The Music Got Me"

The late rapper Tupac Shakur made a profound statement in 1995 while he was incarcerated at Clinton Correctional Facility, a Maximum-Security prison in upstate New York. In an interview, he stated, "...My music is spiritual if you listen to it...I tell my innermost darkest secrets. I reveal myself in every one of my records, from 'Dear Mama' to 'Shed so Many Tears', I tell my own personal problems...[then he goes on to say]...Don't just bob your head to the beat, peep the game, listen to what I'm saying and hold us [rappers] accountable for it...."

Look closely at the following lyrics from Pac's song, "*Shed So Many Tears*":

> I couldn't see it; I had a mind full of demons trying to break free
>
> They planted seeds in my head and they hatched, sparking the flame, Inside my brain like a match, such a dirty game, This ain't the life for me, I WANNA CHANGE."

Why am I bringing this up? Because for me, as I began to transition in life, music was a pivotal aspect. You see, I wasn't, and still am not, just into listening to music. I study the lyrics of artists, their backgrounds, tap into who they are, what they are saying, even engaging the evil that may be connected to what they had to do to make a hit record, so much so that the music became ingrained in my soul, becoming a part of me, a part of my very being.

I would go to sleep listening to rap music, wake up to rap music, listen to it throughout the day and love watching music videos on BET (Rap City, Uncut, etc.) and MTV and reading Hip-Hop music magazines like *XXL*, *The Source*, *Vibe* and *Word-up*!

In all honesty, Hip-Hop also became a learning tool for me, similar to how people see pimps, drug dealers, and all types of hustlers in their neighborhoods as role models who may teach them the game and they listen to them because they respect them and their hustle; such was the impact of hip-hop artist in my personal life, of which, through their words and lyrics, they were teaching me the game and being role models to me for the life I was beginning to live.

As I jumped headfirst in the "game", it was then that I began to learn from the streets, and friends I had history with that were already in the streets, but at first, I learned through the music.

Hip-Hop was everything to me, even a comforting mechanism when I would become extremely angry. Music artist like Tupac, who was murdered at 25, Nas, Mobb Deep, Bone-Thugs-n-Harmony, Young Jezzy, especially the song "Hypnotize" off the album called "*The Inspiration*," Lil' Wayne, and BG and the rest of the Hot Boys, who, while I was later in prison, inspired me to get my fingers tattooed with the words "Hot Boi" since I was living that type of lifestyle that they rapped about and were labeled after.

Also people like Mac of No Limit Records, who was incarcerated for a manslaughter charge, being sentenced to 30 years; Soulja Slim, who got murdered at 25 in New Orleans; C-Murder, who is serving a life-sentence for murder; UGK (Underground Kings), one of whose members, Pimp-C, died from a Cocaine overdose; DJ Screw of the Screwed-up Click from Houston, Texas, who died from an overdose of "Syrup,"; and so many other rappers that I felt and feel speak on the rawness of street life, that would, through their music teach me and calm me when I was upset, or bring out more of my rage and anger when ready to fight or do something negative. Music was in me on another level then it is for most casual listeners.

I became like the rappers I was listening to, adopting style of dress, language, and actions, becoming possessed by whatever spirit was in the particular songs.

My dad once told me that he knew that I was possessed with demons while living my life doing what I wanted to do. He knew he had to continue to pray for me and my freedom, of which my incarcerations were physical, spiritual and mental, but the fact of the matter was that I was responsible for allowing those demons in, especially since I immersed myself in the depths of the music, and to break free from those demons I would have to let go of certain things and find my identity and freedom in Christ instead of being shackled to the music; but it would be years before I could.

For ten to twelve years, I dabbled on the Devil's playground in many areas of my life, and the devil had no intentions of letting me go easy!

I feel that the music was in me so much that in my 20's I had gotten a tattoo on the right side of my face, which I believe was more than a mere tattoo, I believe that it was also the demons inside of me beginning to manifest themselves on my face through something I, and those around me, were familiar with. It was a "Cry Later" face of the "Smile Now, Cry Later Faces," with more of an evil face than a face that's in tears.

My ex-wife told me that the first night that I had gotten the tattoo, that she rolled over in the middle of the night and got scared because she saw this evil face on my face with red eyes, looking at her, feeling like evil was staring directly at her. The tattoo symbolized my inner face showing how I felt inside; the pain, the diabolicalness, the hate, the frustration, the demons!

My ex-wife also explained to me that one night, as I was in a drunken rage, she saw my face distort and contort taking on another form, an evil satanic form. I was possessed by devils, and for years had been inviting them in and allowing them to have full sway over my life. No, I didn't do a séance or play with a Ouija board to allow them in; I simply was possessed, which for me, I believe in part, came through what I was listening to.

"I can't change, it's the music, and it's got me." I spoke these words a few years before God got my attention, and within my personal life, I can attest to the fact that Tupac was right; Hip-Hop Music is spiritual, but just like with anything, we have to ask ourselves, what's the spirit connected to what we are engaging in?

Years ago, I didn't just "bob my head to the music", I became a lot of what my favorite artist rapped about and things kept on getting worse for me.

JailLyfe: Jesus Always Is Looking
Love Your Friends & Your Enemies

Terminology Defined

Chapter 6:

Triple Gold D's-A Gold Dayton Rim for Your Car

Candy-Coated Drippin' Wet Paint-A Type of Paint Job Done to a Car that Gives it a Glossy Look

12's in the Trunk-Size of Speakers in the Trunk of Your Vehicle

JailLyfe: Jesus Always Is Looking
Love Your Friends & Your Enemies

Chapter Six

"The House Party"

I was 15 years old in the summer of 1998 and that was when life for me definitely began to take an even more drastic turn. The previous school year, I had been expelled from a Seventh-day Adventist boarding academy in the ninth grade and had to finish the remainder of the year at a private SDA School in San Marcos, TX. I dreaded this, mostly because I was already fed up with school and had no goals since my sports dreams were crushed! All I wanted to do now was make money and talk to females, while watching a lot of BET music videos, being drawn towards the flashy cars, half-naked women, and money that would be flaunted throughout the videos, along with the high priced cars I would see, leading me to fantasize about getting a 1964 drop-top Impala on some tripled gold "D's", with blue, candy-coated drippin' wet paint, Cocaine leather white interior, and a couple of 12's in the trunk.

I was slowly but surely being sucked into living another lifestyle, loving everything that came with this "new" type of life for me.

Close to the end of the school year of 1997 and 1998, we moved to San Antonio, TX, the city that taught me so much more about the streets and the third largest city in Texas, behind Houston and Dallas.

My spiral down into this new type of life-style continued, therefore by this time I wanted to experiment with drinking and drugs since I had heard so much about them from some of my cousins and friends that would smoke weed and drink alcohol, coupled with being influenced by the music I had been looking at, listening to, and emulating. However, I didn't have a reliable source near me to get what I wanted, and most people around me were into sports as opposed to drugs, and those that I trusted to get me what I wanted, friends and family, lived in other cities, yet they were heavily involved with narcotics on many levels, from using to selling.

That summer a friend of mine's older sister had a house party around the corner from where we lived. My brother and I were invited to this party, which did not start until late in the night, like most parties. The plan was that once our parents were good and asleep, we would sneak out the window and drive over to the party. Sounded like a good plan to us!

We made it to the party maybe around midnight or a little sooner. Being that we grew up in a household that did not party or dance, and never having been to a school dance function, actual attempts at dancing and having to display rhythm was foreign to us, those that understand the struggle can relate. Nevertheless, we were bent on going to the party and I was determined that I was going to try alcohol for the first time in my life.

That night I drank a good deal of liquor and beer, even though I didn't know what kind of alcohol I was actually drinking. In addition, I also smoked tobacco from a Philly or Swisher Sweet Cigar, of which this also was my first time. While there were people at the party smokin' weed, I didn't try any that night, but it was just a couple days away before I would smoke my first blunt.

That night I got so drunk that I was stumbling everywhere, very much disoriented. I remember my dad coming up to the party and finding us there and taking us back to the house, being extremely upset. Boy, was he mad at us!

The next morning, I had a severe hangover, but even though I was vomiting and had a terrible headache, I knew that this was the life that I wanted to live. The alcohol provided a carefree attitude and seemed to drown out my frustrations for the moment, plus it was fun!

"Where Am I Headed?"

On the night of the house party, years before I reached the legal age for drinking, I began to find comfort in alcohol. A couple of days later, I told one of my cousins, who had already been smoking weed for years, about the house party, and that I had tried drinking and smoking tobacco for the first time. He was excited and happened to have some weed with him that day. What a coincidence, right? My cousin asked me if I wanted to get high. I said, "Of course." My first experience with marijuana was a great one and I was hooked!

As a teenager, I liked the feeling of being high, feeling like I was in another realm of life. I also liked inhaling the weed smoke, then blowing it out of my nose and mouth seeing everything seemingly start to move in slow motion.

Despite being upset that my dreams were not going to come to fruition, life was now becoming attractive again, but this time through my distorted vision of weed smoke and alcohol; this was the life for me, and I knew it! I was hooked, and for years I would continue my spiral downhill, dealing with many bad situations and negative emotions eventually leading me to use other types of drugs.

JailLyfe: Jesus Always Is Looking
Love Your Friends & Your Enemies

Terminology Defined

Chapter 7:

Reppin'-Representing Where One is from Based on Colors and Gangs Signs

Knuckle up & Thrown Down-Get Ready to Fight

Ratted-To Tell on Someone

Heated-Mad/Angry/Upset

JailLyfe: Jesus Always Is Looking
Love Your Friends & Your Enemies

Chapter Seven

"Juvenile Detention Center"

"Don't let anyone take your food!"

Those were the words my friend told me as we were being handcuffed, separated, and headed to different juvenile facilities.

It was December of 1998, and I was 16 years old. My homeboy, a member of the Bloods gang, had done time before, but for me, this was my first time. I had heard of TYC, Texas Youth Commission, which is dubbed as "Gladiator School" because the people doing time at a TYC facilities are all youth and feel like they have something to prove to each other through fighting. At TYC facilities, there are youngsters from all over Texas, creating a blend of young aggression, reppin' different cities and hoods, with a strong gang element, ranging from the Crips, the Bloods, the Mexican Mafia, and the many other street gangs in Texas. This is generally a recipe for combat, and a new arrival had better be ready to knuckle up and "throw down" as soon as he got there.

Although knowing this information as I headed to a juvenile facility in East Texas, I didn't know really what to expect. I just knew that my homeboy told me, "Don't let anyone take your food," and I was ready to defend myself by all means necessary!

The crimes that I was being charged with were burglary of a habitation, assault on a police officer, and resisting arrest. When the police came to get me at school, I had been drinking Hennessey all that morning. Also, I had just finished fighting with a teacher and a student that had "ratted" on us for stealing over $500.00 from some college students that were visiting our school for a gymnastics program.

A couple of days before I was arrested, the police had come to the school to investigate the theft. I was one that was being interrogated, and since I was a suspect because a student had snitched on us, I was instructed to refrain from attacking the student or doing anything that would cause the student harm or get me in trouble while the investigation was open.

I was heated when I eventually saw the boy that had told on us. He was accompanied by a teacher that was supposed to be protecting him. But without even thinking, I immediately ran up to him and swung on him with my right fist, connecting the punch to his face, which caused the teacher to jump on my back, while the student ran off.

With the liquor still flowing in my system and heightening my anger, I tried to inflict pain on the teacher. I wrestled him off my back, then got on top of him and began to slam his head into the ground several times, which caused him to use the bathroom on himself out of fear. I then let him go and headed for the student, wherever he had gone. I was completely out of control at this point, and unable to control my raging anger! When I found him, I began to attack him but was hindered by a couple of people jumping on me and holding me down.

Finally, when two police officers arrived, a burly male and a female officer approached me and several things happened quite fast, as I was not interested in being arrested. I swung on one of the officers but before you knew it, I was wrestled to the ground, and the police had me face down in the mud like they were about to hog-tie me and throw me somewhere with the cattle.

This was my very first time in handcuffs and my very first time headed to being locked up. However, this was not my first time stealing and breaking the law, just my first time being caught and committing a crime of this magnitude.

At the young age of around seven or eight, I can remember beginning my habits of stealing. It started out with small things like candy and toys from stores and small amounts of money from my parents. Over the years, I progressed into bigger things.

"Locked Up"

Immediately after I was booked in, with things like my fingerprints and picture taken (mug shot), I was permitted to take a shower. Then I was taken to my cell. At this point I had no idea how long I would be locked up since the Burglary of a Habitation crime was considered a 2nd Degree Felony and carried a sentence of 2-20 years in prison. Can you imagine doing 20 years in prison? There's a saying in the criminal world that goes like this: "You do the crime; you do the time." That can be a pretty harsh reality when you are facing many years in prison, but it's all part of the street game.

I was taken to a single man cell that was isolated from the other young offenders, then after 24 hours in the isolation tank, I was taken to my permanent cell, where I would spend 23 hours a day on lock down in a single man cell.

Since I had not been sentenced as yet, I was not permitted contact with the youth that were serving their sentences already. Along with me in my cellblock area were several other young people that had not been sentenced, but who had to stay in their cells for 23 hours a day also. The hour in which I got to get out of my cell for the day was pretty much split between eating lunch and dinner in the chow hall with the others in my cellblock area, and occasionally we would be permitted to get a few minutes of rec. time in the gym to play basketball or go to a class to do some schoolwork that your school would send over for you to do.

Notice that I said that we would come out of our cells for lunch and dinner and not breakfast. Breakfast was at 5:30 in the morning, and it was brought to your cell. You would have to wake up, eat your food before a server would come back around to collect your tray, then you could go back to sleep or do whatever you planned on doing. However, whatever you decided to do, you would have to do it in your cell because the next time your door would open would be either for you to go use the bathroom or for lunch time.

This was very hard for me. I've always been a very active person and having to sit in a small room all day for 23 hours with concrete walls on all four sides, a window too high for me to be able to see through, (I started to be able to tell time by where the sun's glare would shine through my cell window) and a thin plastic mattress, thin plastic pillow, and a white sheet for bedding, was a hard adjustment but this was part of the life I was livin'!

I would try to read the Bible to pass time and understand more of who God really was but had such a difficult time understanding the Bible because all I was given was the King James Version, which all of the Old English conversation in the Bible didn't make sense to me, therefore it was easy for me to give up.

Also, in the juvenile center, to pass the time, I would find myself reading ghost stories and other books so that I could just have something to help occupy my time in my single man cell.

I remember my parents coming to the juvenile center and visiting me behind the glass that separated us. On the other side of the glass and now in the hands of the state, I looked into their eyes and saw their deep hurt. You see, when you break the law and get caught, you no longer belong to your mothers and fathers; you belong to the state. No matter how much your mom cries and wants to hold you at the end of the visit, you have to go back to your cell, while your family goes back home, and the state does with you what they feel is best. It's a terrible feeling, and I hope you who are reading this book will never have to experience it. But "If you do the crime," young people, be prepared to "do the time." And remember that when you do time, your whole family does time with you.

I ended up spending a week in the facility before being released and eventually going to court. Since it was my first offense, I was given a year of juvenile probation without having to serve any more detention center time. Boy, was I happy! But my mind hadn't changed as of yet.

After the verdict, I was back in San Antonio, TX, back to hanging out, and back to smoking weed, even while on probation. Little did I know that less than a year would pass before I would be charged with a second felony while still on probation for the first charge.

But this time I would be charged as an adult!

JailLyfe: Jesus Always Is Looking
Love Your Friends & Your Enemies

Terminology Defined

Chapter 8:

Tank-Holding Cell Before being Processed into Permanent Housing Cellblock

Ol' School Car-Car's that are Generally from years like the 1950s and Earlier to 1980s, Give or Take

System in the Trunk-Speakers and Amplifier for Louder Sound of Music in the Vehicle

Tatted Up-Having Lots of Tattoos on your Body

Get it How You Live-A Phrase that Means you do What you Have to do Based on How you are Living

JailLyfe: Jesus Always Is Looking
Love Your Friends & Your Enemies

Chapter Eight

"Jail"

October 30th, 1999, Halloween Eve, and the tank was filling up fast. I was in the Berrien County Jail, across the river from Benton Harbor, Michigan, a place known for heavy gang activity, that holds connections with Chicago's infamous South and West sides.

I had just turned seventeen—27 days before my incarceration. This was my second time being locked up, but this time I was facing an adult charge, which was called 2nd Degree Home Invasion, carrying a maximum sentence of fifteen years in prison.

Fifteen years!

What in the world was I doing? Less than a year before, I had been incarcerated at a juvenile facility in Texas facing a maximum sentence of twenty years, and now I was in a jail with adults in Southwestern Michigan facing another serious charge!

How in the world did I get there?

"The Move from Texas to Michigan"

This move went against everything that I wanted to do. I had finished my 10th grade year at *Theodore Roosevelt High School* in San Antonio, Texas. How I passed the 10th grade, to this day I have no clue. You see, during the very first week of the first semester of my 10th grade year, I had gotten suspended for two weeks. I came back from my suspension, but a couple months later I was suspended again for four days for smoking marijuana on school grounds. Then after that suspension I came back, and in December of 1998 I was incarcerated in an East Texas juvenile Center.

The second semester of school began with me back in public school and having no interest in academics. Why? Because I was bent on gettin' fast money and all the "finer" things that come along with it, such as getting gold teeth in the mouth, which is a big thing down south. It may not be attractive to some, but I loved it!

The 2nd semester of my 10th grade year, I would go to school and see young dudes my age, sixteen and seventeen, coming to school with gold teeth in their mouths, an ol' school car with a system in the trunk, and tatted up! I thought to myself, "What in the world are these dudes doin' to get so much money?" When I found out, hands down I was head first in it! Time to really "jump off the porch" as the sayin' goes. I discovered that these young dudes were "hustlin": sellin' drugs, robbin', pimpin' and living by the phrase, "Get it how you live".

To see youngsters making more money in a day than your moms or pops make in a month was very alluring and attractive to me. Already I was smoking weed and drinking alcohol, but this hustling thing was so much more attractive, and smoking and drinking were just a part of this type of lifestyle it seemed, so it was what it was. To me, it was like one activity complimented the other.

I spent most of my second semester of my 10th grade year skipping school, messing with females, drinking and smoking, and being in ISS (In School Suspension) or Saturday school. Saturday school was for those who skipped or missed so many days throughout the school year that they would have to go to school on Saturday for about four or five hours to make up for the lost days. The only reason I went is that my parents made me go; other than that, I could have cared less about going.

In reality though Saturday school was kind of like a family reunion. Students that you wouldn't see for a while because they constantly skipped school would meet there and join in laughing and talking about how ridiculous we thought school was.

School at this point seemed extremely pointless. I had no legitimate plans for the future and couldn't see beyond the day. It was no point of asking me what my plans were in five years because you probably wouldn't have liked my answer. All that my mind could fathom was money, money, money! "Why go to school for all those years just to have a "rinky, dink" type of job?" was what I thought. Also, the subjects the schools were teaching me had no relevance to what I desired to do.

I remember one time my dad asking my brother and me what we wanted to do when we got older. My brother began to spout all this fantastic stuff that parents love to hear, because he has always had his head on his shoulders better than I have, and then it was my turn to speak, and as most young people who can't see past the day, all I could state was that I wanted to do was buy a car. That's what my future was bent on, getting a car! Why? So, I could ride around the city all day and night and do whatever I desired. I loved San Antonio!

The 10th grade taught subjects like biology, which I knew I would never use in life. It taught subjects like keyboarding, world history, and geometry, which I definitely knew was beyond pointless for what I wanted to do in life. The only thing I wanted to know was measurements for drugs, like grams, ounces, and pounds! Everything else seemed irrelevant. Besides, I knew how to count, how to read, and pretty much all the basics; I thought I was good to go. School is not designed to teach you the streets, and the streets are not designed to teach you what school has to offer. These are two different worlds. All I wanted was street knowledge, which I eventually got, and school could not teach it to me. So why be there? With these feelings, I easily decided that I would not go to school that often.

So, you see where my thinking was and why I say I don't know how I passed the 10th grade!

"Back to the Move"

Towards the end of the summer, my dad had moved to Andrews University in Berrien Springs, Michigan, where I had been born, to take a class in flying. My brother was headed off to Southwestern Adventist University (SWAU) for his freshman year of college, my mother was not comfortable with my staying in San Antonio with just her since at this point I was not listening to her as a parent, so I was sent to Michigan to be with my dad. At this point I was rebellious to the core: smoking weed, staying out in the city all night, refusing to listen, and so much more. I thought that at sixteen I was a man and that I knew everything and didn't need parents to tell me anything. They just seemed too restrictive, and I wanted to be my own parent. So, my parents easily decided that it would be best for me to go to Michigan. Boy, did I hate this move!

Before I left Texas to go to Michigan, I made sure that I left Texas with some weed; I didn't know what Michigan had to offer on the marijuana tip, but I was definitely gonna take a couple of blunt's worth of weed with me to smoke when I got there. I hated everything about this move that I was being "forced" to make and I was about to make somebody pay for moving me from Texas to Michigan.

I was already "off the porch" and involved in illegal activities, but now I was about to link up with some Vice Lords and GD's that had been active in the streets putin' in work as the saying goes. These dudes were young, bout makin' money by any means necessary, and were willing to "give me the game" even more-so then I knew at this point; and I was ready to take it all in!

Terminology Defined

Chapter 9:

Prison Boot Camp-Where First Time Offenders were often sent which Involved very Rigorous Activities Similar to the Military

Halfway House-Place Sentenced which Prepares you to go Back into Society

Blunt Session-Smoking Multiple Blunts of Weed with others in One Sitting

40 oz. Malt Liquor-The Size of the Bottle Containing the Malt Liquor which is Stronger than Beer but Weaker than Liquor

Hittin' a Lick-A Robbery or Some Type of Illegal Come Up

Chapter Nine

"Hangin' with the Gangsta's"

The move was supposed to be only for a year, and then I would be able to go back to Texas. At that point I didn't know that I would spend about 9 months of that year in some form of incarceration: jail, prison boot-camp, a half-way house for thirty days, and three months of house arrest, the last of which, to me, was worse than jail. But I guess due to my mentality, personal decisions at the time and the people I hung with, I was setting myself up for failure. In jail there's a saying that goes, "You came on vacation, but you left on probation." I didn't come to Michigan on vacation per se, but I was definitely going to be leaving on probation.

A few days after I had gotten to Michigan, I met someone who would become one of my good friends even to this day, I'll call "G" (street nickname changed and real name not mentioned). We were the same age but he had strong gang ties.

I was later introduced to others that I eventually hung around with and who were a part of G's opposing street gang, yet we were all cool. "G" and I hit it off immediately, since we listened to the same music, such as UGK, Cash Money, and many others. On top of that, we both smoked weed and drank alcohol, so that was more than enough to have in common as a teenager goin' through life's struggles.

The very first day that we met, we were engrossed in a "blunt session," where we mixed the marijuana that I had brought with me from Texas with some Michigan marijuana that he had. That was a potent combination! Our "infamous" friendship began with a blunt session!

The day that I met "G" and we smoked together was also the first day of school registration. I was there in Michigan as an 11th grader, but boy, did I start the school year off wrong! I didn't care about school anyway so it didn't matter to me!

My eyes were bloodshot red from the high, and I wasn't focused on doing right by any means. Several things were not going to allow me to finish out my schooling or aid me in doing the right thing anyhow. One, my mentality was on fast money; two, someone or somebody was going to pay for moving me against my will to Michigan; three, I started off registration "high as a kite;" and four; I was linked up with the right people who were about the wrong things like myself.

In August of 1999 I began my 11th grade year and ended up going to two separate schools in a matter of 2 months, of which combined, I probably attended school one week spread out over a 2-

month period before getting incarcerated. School was just nowhere on my mind! I would go there solely with the purpose of stealing some money from someone so that I could go and get some weed to smoke or some cheap alcohol and 40 ounces of Malt liquor to drink.

We would consume alcohol like Paul Masson, a cheap "hood" wine called MD 20/20, E & J (Erk & Jerk/Easy Jesus) brown liquor, Wild Irish Rose, "OE", Schlitz Malt Liquor, coupled with a lot of weed smokin' and runnin' through at least a pack a day of black-n-mild's, which I smoked before I got heavy into cigarettes. All of this at 16 years old! I was destroying my mind and body at a young age, but this is the typical lifestyle of those whose lives I was emulating, so I justified it by it feeling that this was the norm.

As stated, at this point-n-time I was smoking a lot of marijuana which was the motivating factor that led me to get my first tattoo at 16 years old. It was done with a home-made tattoo gun and reads "Weed & Money," displaying a weed leaf and a dollar sign on my right shoulder. You see, I was addicted to weed and obsessed with gettin' fast money so what better then to get "inked up" with what I loved!

Within a little more than two months of my being in Michigan, I was incarcerated and facing my first adult charge. Since I had gotten to Michigan, I became involved in a lot of theft and the breaking & entering's (B&E's) of houses around town. From this hustle, I would make pretty ok money for someone who was only sixteen and seventeen. Each night we would find ourselves in a different house, stealing someone else's stuff that they had worked hard for.

"The Night that I was Arrested"

It was early in the morning, maybe around 2 to 3am, when the police came banging on the apartment door where my dad and I lived. Three of my homeboys and I had recently returned from trying to get into a club that night, but "G" and I were too young to get in, so we turned around and came home. That was fine with me because I was so high and drunk by the time we got to the club that I could hardly function.

One reason I was so "messed up" was that before going to the club, three of us had "hit a couple of licks" at some houses for a few hundred dollars and we were partially celebrating, which led to us wanting to cap off the night by goin' to the club.

Periodically after hittin' a lick, especially if it was major, we would try to find some way to celebrate, like gettin' an ounce of weed and smokin' it, going to the mall to spend money, or going out somewhere fancy to eat—something a little different than what we would do on a day-to-day basis. Little did we know, we had been under surveillance by the police for a while and they had been watching us at the apartment where we hung out, but I didn't find this out until after I was arrested.

The night we were arrested, prior to our going to the club, we had brought some of the stolen goods back to the apartment of someone I'll call "Big J" (Street name changed). Since he had his own spot, this is mainly where we would all hang out. But when we had returned from tryin' to get into the club and had gone to our separate houses, the police at some point knocked on the door of "Big J." When he opened the door, the police were able to peek enough inside to see the stolen goods sitting on his living room floor! Being that this particular house was under surveillance, the police already knew what was inside, regardless, why "Big J" opened the door with all that stolen stuff in plain view, I don't know!

Now that they had gotten "Big J," they were coming for me next, oh snap!

Terminology Defined

Chapter 10:

Shank-Prison Weapon

Meth Lab-A Place for Making

Methamphetamine Drugs

Cell Dayroom-Area where Inmates in that

Cell Block could Congregate

CO's-Corrections Officers

The Hole-An Isolated Segregation Cell

away from other Inmates

JailLyfe: Jesus Always Is Looking
Love Your Friends & Your Enemies

Chapter Ten

"Charged as an Adult"

At the beginning of chapter eight, I started out telling you about being in the holding cell on Halloween Eve in 1999. Here is the rest of that story...

It would be a few days before I was processed and classified to what cell block area I would be assigned. Since I had come to jail late Saturday night and classification usually took place once a week on a weekday, it meant that I would have to wait until Tuesday to be able to go to my permanent cell block area. Imagine a room, like the average sized bedroom, then picture up to twenty-three people in that room, surrounded by grey concrete walls and hard concrete floors, one toilet for everybody, all of whom could see you use the bathroom, and no shower! This was the holding cell I was in from Saturday night until Tuesday afternoon when I was classified. Talk about miserable! People would be in there that were drunk, having drug addiction withdrawals, or simply just high from whatever narcotic they were on when they were arrested; a fist fight or a shank slashin' could go down at any time so you better be ready for any and everything any given second!

Three of us were taken to jail for the crime we had committed that night.

As time was being issued out, I learned that "Big J" had done twelve days in the county jail and I would be given a total of nine months in different forms of incarceration along with three years of probation, and the third person, an older cat and a long time Vice-Lord who had been to prison before, received a year's worth of prison time behind the crime we committed since he was the only one who had previous adult violations; mine was only the previous juvenile offense and to my knowledge, "Big J" had never been in any form of physical incarceration up to this point.

In the street game there are codes that are lived by. One being, you don't snitch! All I can say is that street codes weren't followed in the cases between the three of us and time got issued out by the State of Michigan. But I don't have hard feelings towards anyone for anything.

I was finally classified and placed in a cell block area with some dudes facing major sentences. One guy was in for allegedly murdering his wife with a hammer, another faced ninety-nine years for operating a Meth lab, others had charges similar to mine, and still others were in for charges related to drugs and/or conspiracy.

While I was in the county jail, I had gotten into two fights. The second fight wasn't really a fight in every sense of the word, it was more of an attempt to gain respect and signal to others that I could handle myself. You see, this older inmate who had done penitentiary time before had tried to clown me by saying that when I got to prison other inmates would put Kool-aid on my lips, take my manhood by raping me and turn me into a prison female because my lips are naturally kind of red. That was disrespect, and this particular thing I couldn't let it ride or I would be viewed as a punk! Not about to happen!

Incarceration can be a lot about showing no fear, gaining respect, and handling yourself. I understood this, so I immediately grabbed the guy who talked about making me a female by the head and ran his head into the side of the steel bed in his cell. After that incident, he had told others that I could handle myself and that I was not weak, even though I was always one of the smaller persons wherever I was incarcerated.

The actual fight that I had gotten into was over a simple chess game. I was just learning how to play chess, and the person I was playing with was talking all types of trash to me since he was beatin' me. I'm the type of person that talks a lot of junk as well, no matter if I am losing or winning at a game, so I retaliated by cussin' at him, which caused tensions to escalate leading us to face off and fight.

Within a split second, I had stepped back from him and had taken my shirt off because I didn't want him to be able to grab a hold of it while we were fightin'. While he was still talking, I snuck him with a right blow straight to the nose. I hit him so hard, instantly blood came rushing out of his nostrils onto the floor of the cell dayroom. We began to tussle a little bit, and once I had gotten him to the ground, I quickly stood up over him, ready to jump on him to stomp him into the concrete. But while I was in midair jumping and about to come down on top of him, the guy that was incarcerated on a murder charge in my cell area grabbed me out the air and ended the fight. Since I was cool with pretty much everyone in the cell block area, when the COs came to investigate the situation, everyone vouched for me, saying that I was just defending myself. Since everyone vouched for me, the person with whom I had been fightin' was taken to the "hole", but I was permitted to continue my time in the same cell area.

Fights are a reality when incarcerated. There are many more stories I could tell you about prison violence that I witnessed and heard about: people getting their food taken and being spat in the face because they showed weakness by crying; people getting into fights all hours of the day or night because one wants to talk while others want to sleep; people violently approaching others for sexual favors; and on and on. There's a lot I could tell you because it's a very real reality you don't want to face! But keep this in mind, "If you do the crime, be ready to do the time."

I remained in the county jail for about a month and a half, and then was sentenced to two and a half to four and a half years in prison, but that was canceled due to the offense being my first adult crime. The judge ended up giving me three months of prison boot camp, then one month in a half-way house, and finally three months of house arrest. A few days after I was sentenced, I was shipped off to *Camp Cassidy Lake Prison Boot Camp* in Michigan in the dead of winter. I was not ready for it, but I had to complete the program by all means necessary because if you failed out of the program, you would be sent back to your sentencing county. The prison sentence that was canceled due to your going to boot camp would be reinstated, plus doubled due to your failure in the program. That meant my two-and-a-half to four-and-a-half-year sentence would turn into a four-and-a-half to eight-and-a-half-year prison sentence.

What would boot camp have to offer, and would I make it through? Keep reading to find out.

Terminology Defined

Chapter 11:

P.T.-Physical Training

GED-General Equivalency Diploma

Play the System-Manipulate Things

JailLyfe: Jesus Always Is Looking
Love Your Friends & Your Enemies

Chapter Eleven

"Prison Boot Camp"

"You address me as 'Sir' when you talk to me, boy;" "Sound off, boy;" "Only thing that comes from Texas are steers and Queers, and I don't see no horns on you, so you must be a queer!" The guards would get on my nerves on a regular basis with comments like these. They would curse you out on a regular basis, seemingly trying to instigate inmates to act rashly! This would happen to everyone quite frequently in several differing forms. But due to my mouth, it happened to me a lot. In fact, one incident took place where I had been choked by a guard for not sounding off. These Co's would be ex-military people, and while boot camp for the military is filled with yelling and cursing, they seemed to have extra aggression towards us. In their eyes, because we were inmates, we had violated the law instead of going to military boot camp on our own free will to serve our country. So, they seemed to let it be known, to some of us at least, that we were the scum of the earth.

When you first get to boot camp, no matter what kind of facial hair or hairstyle you had, everyone got the same raggedy Chile bowl haircut. This thing is not stylish by any means; your hair is patchy, as the Chile bowl is uneven and unprofessionally done. The haircut takes all of 30 seconds to be over with. Then they have you hold your inmate number up on a board of some sort, and proceed to take your mugshot. While all of this is going on, there are several guards, all of them big and tall, yelling and screaming in your face, with spit flying everywhere.

Intake day was crazy, but for the first few days we were considered "ghosts", all geared up in white jumpsuits and helmets tryin' to make it the first couple of days while everything was new and fresh, scary and weird!

But though you are called a "ghost" when you first get there, you are by no means unseen.

Throughout the three-month program, I was placed in handcuffs many times. It started with my first three weeks in Alpha company due to my talking back to the guards, refusing to perform as they wanted me to, and overall, just being young and dumb with a motor mouth.

After three weeks of going through what seemed like Hell on Earth, I learned my lesson. But it was the hard way. In prison boot camp there's something called "the motivation squad." If a person didn't seem to be motivated enough because of their behaviors, they could get placed in an orange vest and would have to do extra hard work throughout the day.

Basically, not following the rules the way you were supposed to was defined as a lack of motivation, and if the guards deemed that you fit that description then you would be on the motivation team. Of course, I found myself on the motivation squad at least once, maybe twice.

If you have seen the movie *First Time Felon* with Treach, of the rap group *Naughty by Nature*, and Omar Epps, then you have a visual idea of what prison boot camp is like. It can be very hard and rigorous.

On the motivation squad, we would do stuff like move a pile of rocks from one area to another area, having to carry two full buckets of rocks with us everywhere we went in both hands. Talk about heavy and tiresome and you were not allowed to place the buckets down at all unless instructed. Other than that, you had to carry the buckets everywhere. If you got caught placing your bucket down, then everyone on the squad would have to pay by doing some hard P.T. for your mess-up. And, boy, would people be mad at you if you were the cause of them having to do some P.T. Talk about a way to make people hate you!

When you have a person on the squad that likes to play and act out, which could get everyone in trouble, then you have a problem on your hands. You have to understand that on the squad, you are not only accountable to yourself but to others as well, and many fights could break out in that tense atmosphere. Several fights did take place while I was there, because of one person wanting to "act out". This experience was kind of like the sports shirt that says, "There's no 'I' in team".

Anyhow, the daily schedule at the Prison Boot Camp was grueling. Wake-up was at 5 a.m., and breakfast was at 6 a.m., but, as with all of the other meals, you only had about three minutes to eat everything. You couldn't look around while you ate, and couldn't talk with others either. Imagine having a whole plate of food to eat and only three minutes to do it in. Talk about a serious case of indigestion! From breakfast we would go to work, which sometimes consisted of shoveling snow in the dead of the Michigan winter, or moving piles of leaves or rocks—whatever they could think of to occupy your time, but was I freezing my butt off! Texas does not have winters like Michigan, and it was my first time experiencing a winter like this that I could remember.

We would work until around lunchtime, when we would have another three minutes to eat. After eating lunch would be the general P.T. time, and for about an hour or so, we would be doing every exercise imaginable. After P.T. was school. While I was there, I received my GED, which I laughingly called the Good Enough Diploma. After school was dinnertime, with another three minutes to eat your food, which meant for the entire day you had a total of nine minutes for eating three meals. Then we would do various workouts and drills for the remainder of the day.

There was this one drill called "Santa Bagging." We would take all of our sheets and covers, lay them on the floor, pile all of our belongings into them, tie them up, and then run through the halls with this Santa bag. There wasn't anything Christmas about this thing, just a lot of yelling, screaming, and doing rhythmic cadences. We would have to run with the bags over our heads, out in front of us, and close to us. Talk about a workout, and talk about tiredness at the end of a day!

The days would be exhausting! There was never really any free time; we would always be occupied but the idea was to break us down and build us back up. For most of us, the program really though was just a way to "play" the system and get home.

The way that we as inmates would count down our 12 weeks of being at *Camp Cassidy Lake* was by Snicker bars and sodas. You see, Saturdays were special because in addition to our lunch, we would get a Snicker's Chocolate Candy bar and a soda. So, when someone would come to you and ask, "How much time you got left," your reply would be, "I have eight Snicker Bars to go," meaning that you had eight more weeks of the program to finish. So however, much time you had remaining, most people would answer by Snicker bars instead of weeks. Crazy huh?! But if you have done time you can relate.

I was glad when I got down to having no Snicker bars left before I could get released!

In prison boot camp, you would see grown men using the bathroom on themselves because sometimes the guards would not let them go to the bathroom. During shower time, there were five showerheads in the shower room, with three or four naked grown men to each showerhead. So, there would be fifteen or more men taking a shower at the same time, with shower time consisting of only 30 seconds per group. If anyone was found talking while in the shower, the whole shower time was cut, and you would just go a day without taking a shower.

Boot camp requires much mental strength—with guards spitting on you, yelling at you, getting physical with you from time to time, along with other inmates having built-up aggression and wanting to fight you. I'm not going to lie and say that these three months were easy, because they weren't! In fact, they were very hard! But after my first three weeks of running my mouth, I began to learn my lesson, and things got a bit easier for me.

My next step after Alpha Company was Bravo Company, and we stayed at this level for 6 weeks, then moved up to Charlie Company for our last three weeks, making everything a total of three months. It was ninety days of pure blood, sweat, tears, and P.T. In fact, there was a cadence that we use to sing while jogging, and it went something like this: "Blood, sweat, tears, and P.T.; that's the life of a going home trainee; blood, sweat, tears, and P.T.; that's the life of a going home trainee."

My three months had finally come. However, my mind was not changed from doing illegal things; in fact, I took boot camp as an opportunity to get healthy and strong for my return back to the same type of things that landed me in incarceration. The program is designed to give you discipline and to break you down and build you up as stated. It's an effective program, but just like anything in life, if you don't want to do right, then all the programs in the world can't help you. Change starts with you! I had a determination to get through the program because I didn't want to go to prison for a lot of years, so I sucked it up and made it through.

My determination to finish the program was not because I saw something wrong within me, as I should have, but it was simply a way to hurry up and get back to the "free world" and fast money that I wanted to make. Only the strong survived that program, and I considered myself one of the strong. You didn't have to be strong physically, but you mainly had to be strong mentally, and I felt that I had that.

Graduation day came in March of 2000. I had come to prison boot camp in December of 1999 and was graduating in the new millennium. Not graduating from high school but graduating through the judicial system. I was in the hands of MDOC, *Michigan Department of Corrections*, and my next transition was to a thirty-day halfway house in Kalamazoo, which I successfully completed. Then it was freedom, but on three months of house arrest, which I would also successfully complete, only going to jail once while on house arrest, which was just a weekend violation. I made it through all of these programs, but my mind was not changed yet. I still had a drive for fast money and my proverbial car was moving with lighting speeds!

Prison, with the big-time felons, was coming real soon but I didn't know how soon until it happened!

Terminology Defined

Chapter 12:

U/A-Urinary Analysis to test for Narcotics

Dirt-Illegal Activities

Trap House-Where Drugs are Sold

Key-Kilogram of Cocaine

Coke-Powdered Cocaine

Big Timer-Someone Respected in the Streets for Selling lots of Drugs and Having lots of Things

Chapter Twelve

"Freedom, but Still Breaking the Law"

Freedom, when generally thought of, is often regarded as being in the physical sense of the word, but truth be told, it can be mental as well. For instance, many people in the outside world can live in a mental prison even though free, on the flip side, many people in physical prisons live in freedom because they are at peace with themselves and their thoughts and actions. Strange but true!

When I was finally released from jail, the prison boot camp, the halfway house, and let off of house arrest all centered around the Home Invasion charge from 1999, I considered myself both mentally and physically free. Whether or not I actually was mentally free didn't matter; I thought I was, but in hindsight I was mentally enslaved for many years. As mentioned in the previous chapter, my mind was not changed. I still had dreams of gettin' rich and I was willing to "Get Rich or Die Tryin" as the rapper 50 Cent says.

Even while I was on house arrest with an electronic ankle bracelet tracking my every move, I was still smokin' weed. Now mind you, I was on three years' probation; I had the ankle bracelet on, which meant that my probation officer could pop up on me anytime; plus, I had to give samples of my urine every single Tuesday for three months while I was on house arrest to test for any narcotics in my system.

I was pushin' it and taking a big chance, but that's the life I lived!

Truth be told, at that point, I didn't really care. Nevertheless, I would be so paranoid when I got high that at times it felt that the thing on my ankle would know that I was high. Talk about freaking out! Every Tuesday before going to give a U/A sample, I would take some pills (Can't tell you the name) and drink about a half a gallon of water which combined, would cause the weed to be "eaten" out of my system. I thought I was being slick! Realize though, that with our actions come consequences. If I had given a dirty U/A, those couple hours of being high would have turned into perhaps months to years behind bars for violating my probation. Was taking those chances really worth it?

Nearing my dad's soon departure from Michigan, and me wanting to go back to Texas, my probation officer at the time had given me an ultimatum. You see, my dad was about to move back to Texas, and then afterwards he and my mother would be moving to South Carolina. I wanted my probation transferred to

Texas so that I could get back there to the state I love so much.

The probation officer stated that the only way I could have my probation transferred was that I either had to go to college full-time or have a job set up to work full-time. Neither of which I was really interested in! I had gotten my GED while incarcerated, so my high school years were done. My brother and a couple of my cousins were in Keene, Texas at Southwestern Adventist University, not too far away from Ft. Worth and Dallas, so I decided to go there, not to learn or acquire higher education—only to get out of Michigan by "playing the system."

After a month or so from when I was released off of house arrest it was time for my dad to leave Michigan, but because of my probation issues, I wasn't able to leave when he left. Being left in Michigan for some time after his departure, I was eventually kicked out of the apartment, then having to ask my homeboy "G" and his mother if I could stay at their house, of which she gave permission.

Imagine, two 17-year-old negros headed nowhere fast that smoked every day and hung out in the streets all hours of the night, which was a daily mixture of youth that would make a lot of bad decisions, from bein' in the hood late at night shootin' dice, ridin' around with a pistol and bullets, drinkin' and smokin' like life had no consequences and being pulled over by police constantly!

Being that I still had not learned my lesson, from being incarcerated I was still doin' dirt, yet my biggest crime up to this point transpired when a homeboy and I did the unthinkable, committing a crime that would cause us to feel like we were kings and rich and on top of the world! It was an out-of-state crime that brought in lots of money. We were able to secure more money than either of us had personally seen in our lives, of which included securing a number of weapons out of the deal as well. Talk about a major risk, but we pulled it off! We were doin' some real street dirt. And I was hooked!

The next day, in order to celebrate we went to a Trap House to get some weed to smoke, of which we had gotten an ounce, then went out to a fancy restaurant to eat and next we went out shopping, spending thousands of dollars like we were "made men" of the mafia. I bought a gold ring, a gold watch, and a gold "piece and chain" spending lots of money like I ain't have a care in this world. I had gotten the Air Jordan 15's that came out in 1999/2000; a brand-new pair of Air Max's that had just come out that year; several other pairs of shoes;

and many clothes, along with a bunch of rap CD's.

And I was only 17 at the time but feeling like I was a millionaire!

My homeboy and I had split the money two ways, straight down the middle and we were ready to take things to another level. We were two teenagers having thousands of dollars in our possession and nobody to tell us anything! I thought I was living my best life!

Back then, at that point, had I known about the drug game from the standpoint of selling instead of just smokin' weed, I would have bought several pounds of Marijuana or invested in a “key” of Coke and started moving it! But it wasn’t until I got to the penitentiary that I would learn the drug game.

Per my probation officer requiring me to go to school fulltime or work full-time for my probation to be transferred to Texas, I began the process of getting into school. Eventually I was accepted into the university, SWAU, by passing the ACT with a score of 14, how I was able to get a 14, to this day I do not know, being that I had slept through the majority of the test and bubbled in anything.

This was my ticket back to Texas, now all I had to do was write a letter to the Universities admittance board, of which I did, and was accepted in and ready to go!

I had done enough hustlin' in order to get back to Texas and by the time I was able to leave Michigan to go to college, based on my probation officer's ultimatum, I had made enough money that I had so many clothes that I could go several weeks without having to wear the same thing twice. To a 17-year-old, you couldn't ask for much else!

I felt like I was a big timer making street power moves, but soon I would yet again be facing a number of years behind bars because of bad decisions! With crime comes consequences!

Terminology Defined

Chapter 13:

Blue Bird-Prison Bus

Shackled-Handcuffed

Bids-Serving Prison time

Maxed Out-To do the Whole Allotted

Sentence of Prison Time One is Given

TDCJ-Texas Department of Criminal

Justice

JailLyfe: Jesus Always Is Looking
Love Your Friends & Your Enemies

Chapter Thirteen

"Penitentiary Bound"

The *Blue Bird* is its name, which looks like the yellow cheese bus we often ride to school which is converted into a prisoner bus, packed full of inmates from varying parts of Texas. We were all shackled in two's next to someone who may have been headed to the penitentiary for some simple repeat offender felony cases to multiple types of murder charges, getting' ready to serve short bids to long-term bids, even life sentences.

Regardless, we were all on the same bus ride together to serve our allotted years of penitentiary time handed down to us between the District Attorney's, Judges and/or Jurors.

On the bus, there were several guards with shotguns, seemingly just waiting to fire them if someone tried to escape, along with caged gates separating various inmates, generally more dangerous ones from the others, or perhaps someone along for the ride about to get released. The bus' windows were mostly covered with steel, so we could barely see through them. We were all headed to Huntsville, the prison capital in Texas, where we would be housed in the Holliday Unit, which was a transfer unit in order to go through diagnostic's testing to see which prison we would be classified, based on things like our IQ, record of violent behavior and crimes.

The name of this unit does not describe the facility by any means. It was full of razor wire and for me, it was a symbol of what my life would look like for a maximum time of five years, age nineteen to twenty-four, if I maxed out on the time I was given. This prison could hold up to a little more than two thousand inmates!

When we first got there, we were unloaded off the bus and taken into a big room that had several TDCJ guards. Every inmate was told simultaneously to strip down out of all of our clothes, getting fully naked, so that we could all be searched, with a room full of prisoners on each side of us. Every single body cavity of an individual had to be searched by the guards to assure that we did not have any drugs or weapons on us.

"Spread your fingers out, open your mouth, lift up your tongue, lift up your feet, wiggle your toes, turn around, bend over, squat, spread your butt cheeks and cough two times". Talk about humiliating!

While this is being done to every inmate, you don't know who is checking you out to try to "turn you out" as a prison female. It's a world where the strong prey on the weak!

I was not a hardened criminal or a violent person; I just had an addiction to fast money, and this addiction finally led me to the penitentiary. I had graduated through the system!

Most people who came from backgrounds like mine tended to grow up and graduate from high school, go to college, and then maybe get their Master's Degree or something equivalent. The extent of their run-ins with the law may only be a minor traffic ticket. But not for me; I was graduating through the judicial system. I had been to a juvenile detention center; been on probation twice; gone to jail, prison boot camp, a halfway house; been on house arrest, and like most I was surrounded by, had not finished traditional high school but had received our GED's while doing time. But now was the moment for me to graduate into the criminal world's university; The penitentiary!

Was I ready for this? What did I do to get here?

JailLyfe: Jesus Always Is Looking
Love Your Friends & Your Enemies

Terminology Defined

Chapter 14:

Hit the Bank-Attempt to Rob it

Off my Rocker-Out of my Mind

Flying Out of the Bank-Running Fast

Arraigned Before a Judge-Crime and Bond Amount is Given

Bond-Amount You Pay to Get Out

Fed vs State Inmates-Federal Inmates are those that have Committed a Federal Crime. State Inmates are those that have Committed a State Crime.

Trustee-Inmate with Good Behavior, so this Type of Inmate gets Special Privileges

Commissary-Prison Store, of which Family and Friends can put Money on your Inmate Account so that You are able

to Buy Items from the Prison Store

Tats-Tattoos

Cat-Person

Paroled-Let out of Prison Early

Fronted-Loaned

Connects-People with Connections to Things

Ride Out-Do my Time

Shady Stuff-Underhanded Actions

JailLyfe: Jesus Always Is Looking
Love Your Friends & Your Enemies

Chapter Fourteen

"The Bank Robbery"

"Man, we hit this bank we could get like 60/70,000 dollars!" Already, two weeks earlier, we had set up and robbed the Subway Restaurant where I worked. The plan was that before I had gotten off work, I would leave a piece of tissue in the back door to the alleyway where we took out the trash. It would close the door, but render it unable to lock. A little bit after we were to shut the store down, the next move would be for my homeboy to come to the store, go through the back door, and hit the register. It was successful!

I ended up getting fired because management suspected that I was involved in the robbery. Even though they were not 100% sure that I was involved, they fired me anyhow, without bringing any legal charges. So that was a plus to me. However, I was eventually jammed up on this robbery but because the bank job outweighed the Subway job, the subway robbery was dropped.

Well, the couple hundred dollars that we had gotten that night were spent really quick, so now it was time to hit another "lick," this time a bank. Prior to hitting the bank that day, I had returned from New Orleans, LA from visiting a certain lady friend.

My homeboy and I had been pumping each other's heads up all day about this robbery. The plan was to wait till between 11pm and 1am to break into the bank, hit the drawers, and then leave with thousands of dollars. The only problem was that we didn't realize that money isn't kept in the bank's drawers at night, instead it's in the vault, securely locked.

While we waited to hit the bank, I was drinking a whole lot of alcohol. To do something this dumb, I definitely could not be sober. I probably had about four to six 40 oz. bottles of Bud Ice beer. I was completely off my "rocker" but still was ready to hit the bank.

Finally, the time came. We gathered up our tools consisting of a couple of screwdrivers and walked over to the bank. Talk about makeshift bank robbers!

We attempted to break in through the back door, but after about 20 minutes of trying to pop the lock, we decided that we needed to find another way in. Mind you, we were not 007 agents so we had no skill at what we were doin'. Dollar signs clouded our minds. Both of us were thinkin' that we should just give up and go home, but neither one of us wanted to confess that we were having these feelings. It wasn't until we were in jail that we voiced that thought. *Interesting!*

So after about twenty minutes we decided to try to throw some rocks through the drive through window to shatter the glass and break in, but we were unsuccessful at this because of how thick the bullet proof glass was.

But our next move was what was going to get us in this bank!

As we walked around to the front, it was like an evil providence was literally about to open the bank doors for us.

Near the main door, lying in the grass directly in front of the bank, there just happened to be a large steel pipe. What a coincidence, right? I immediately grabbed the pipe, knowing that this was our way into the bank, and smashed the front door, shattering the glass. We took off flyin into the bank!

After we had run a few paces, we ended up unknowingly triggering the silent alarm. For all of two minutes we were opening draws looking for the money. Finding nothing, it then dawned upon us that all of the money was safely locked away in the vault; we didn't come out of the bank with any lollipops, envelopes, no money—nothing!

As we were running through the bank, we noticed that many police squad cars were pulling up to the bank extremely fast. Boy, were we in for it! When we came flying out the bank, the only thought on my mind was "I don't plan on gettin' caught!" I was the first one out, and my friend was right behind me. All the police had their guns pointed at us and were yellin', "Freeze!" "Freeze?" I thought, "Yeah, right. Y'all bout to have to work for that money you get paid!" The chase was on. My friend and I got separated; he went one way, and I went another way—and it wasn't until I got to jail the next day that I realized how he had gotten caught that same night.

As I ran in the direction that I took, I glanced behind me and noticed that some police followed him and that others followed me. I've always been a pretty fast runner, so I felt that I had a good chance at outrunning those officers. I remember running towards the woods, or what I thought was the woods; as I was trying to enter those so-called woods, I ran smack into a big tree and hit the ground. Mind you, I still had a lot of alcohol in my system. For a brief second, I was on the ground in the grass and I looked backwards and saw that the police were still chasing me, so I immediately got up and continued running. As I continued to run through an open field in the dark of the night, I ended up falling into something I had not seen—a big ditch full of water! I went under the water, but came up in a matter of seconds, got out of the ditch, took my soaking wet shirt off, then continued to run as hard as

I could but soaking wet. When I looked back this time, the police were nowhere in sight. That didn't stop me from running. I didn't want to get caught, so that thought motivated me to continue running. Man, was I exhausted at this point!

As I continued running to make it back to my apartment, I ended up hopping a barb-wire fence, slicing my ankle on the fence, stealing a bicycle that had two flat tires and handle bars that wobbled off it, but I was tired of running so I needed something.

Finally, I made it home around 3:30 in the morning, exhausted and nervous!

Inside the apartment, I kept all of the lights off and took a shower. I ended up sleeping for a couple of hours and then got up and left the apartment. I figured the police would find out who I was and come looking for me there. Therefore, I left early in the morning, but then came back around 12pm.

After about thirty minutes of being in the apartment, I heard a knock on the door and tiptoed to the peep hole to see who it was. *It was the police.* My heart fell to my toes!

"What am I gonna do?" I quickly thought to myself. I paced around the apartment to look for various places to hide, but none of the spots seemed adequate. So, my next move was to glance out my back window, see if anybody was in the back, and, if no one was, jump out of the window and make a run for it.

When I peeked out, I didn't see anyone, but there was a blind spot, so I would have to go ahead and take a chance. I pushed out the screen and hopped out the window, but as soon as I did, I heard a undercover police say, "Freeze! It's the police." For a split second I had the thought of runnin' and makin' the police attempt to catch me again, but with the gun pointed directly at the back of my head, and the gun cocked ready to shoot, I didn't know if I was willing to take the chance of being shot at close range if I ran off. So, I put my hands up, then placed them behind my back to get handcuffed as instructed, and was taken to the squad car to be transported to the county jail. I knew I was prison bound, no question about it! I was on probation at the time, and this was my second adult felony, so I figured that I would be going down for at least two years in the state penitentiary.

The police already had my friend in custody from the night before. I asked him how he got caught, and he said that he had tried to jump over some bushes while running from the police. He didn't realize that there was barb-wire in between those bushes, so when he tried to "superman" over the bushes, he ended up getting hung-up on the barb-wire. *So much for our plans of getting rich.*

The next day in the county, we were both arraigned before a judge to receive a bond hearing. I just knew that I wasn't getting a bond since I had violated my probation, which would cause a bond hold to be placed on me, and I would have to stay in jail while the sentencing process was going on. To my surprise, I received a $50,000 bond, only ten percent of which had to be paid, so that dropped it down to a $5,000 bond.

When I got back to my cell area, I got on the phone and started making collect calls to see if someone would place my bail. I talked to different family members promising them that if they bonded me out, I would be sure to pay them back every dollar of the money. In the back of my mind, though, the only thought that I had was, "If someone bonds me out, I'm not returning to court!" It was actually better that I stayed in jail because no way was I gonna stay around to go to court on this thing! I would have been on the run, and when you are on the run you cannot live a normal life; mentally I was ok with that. However, everyone I talked to refused to post my bail. The next morning, I was taken back to arraignment and was then told that I had a bond hold. At that moment, I definitely knew that I was not going anywhere knowing that I had to ride out my time.

I remained in the county jail seventy-seven days before I was sentenced. The court-appointed lawyer informed me that the District Attorney wanted to give me ten-years' worth of prison time, but that he had gotten the time down to five years. Immediately, I counted on my fingers, thinking, "Let's see. *Five years, 20, 21, 22, 23, 24.* If I do the whole sentence, I will be twenty-four years old when I will be released." Aloud, I said, "I can do that."

After court I was taken back to my cell block area with the five years I had just received and began mentally preparing to head on out to the penitentiary.

Prison Life

After a week of diagnostics and testing, which included an I.Q. test, HIV/AIDS testing, and classification according to the crime committed, I was sent to a prison in Beaumont, Texas. At that time, this particular prison was divided into federal and state inmates occupying different sides of the prison. Before leaving the Holliday Transfer Unit to head to Beaumont, I remember talking to a young guy who was probably about the same age as I, 19. We had gotten into a brief conversation about how much time we each had and the charges that we were in for. He was the first to begin asking the questions.

"How much time are you in for?" he asked.

"Five years," I replied. "How much time you got?", I then asked.

He answered, "Fifty-years aggravated," meaning that there was a weapon involved in his case and he would have to do at least twenty-five years of his sentence before being eligible for parole.

"What did you do?" I probed.

"Murder," he answered, taking his right hand and sliding his index finger across his neck, showing that he had cut the neck of his victim. *Wow! What in the world have I gotten myself into?* My little ole charge of "Engaging in Criminal Activities" had nothing on what this guy was dealing with! Yet here I was!

From the Holliday Unit, my transfer came through to go to Beaumont not knowing at this point how much of my time I would end up actually doing.

While in Beaumont, I was given a job on the kitchen crew. This was cool with me. In the county jail I was on the kitchen crew as a trustee for a short period of time before being transferred out, and now in prison I was back to my old job.

I was eventually given the job of taking special diet trays around the unit.

This would give me access to not only the state inmates of which I was classified, but the fed inmates as well. After a few days of learning the ropes of this special job and meeting various inmates, I began to use this "diet tray" job as a form of hustle. People would tend to ask me for extra food on their plates or some special kind of food item that they desired but may not be on that day's food list, so I was able to barter with them to get what I wanted by giving them what they wanted. "Aight, you want an extra cup of sugar, that'll be two cigarettes," or it would be stamps, candy, or anything from the Commissary that I desired. In prison, items become money, and these items can be sold to others for favors. In my case, I was trying to gain enough items to pay for some prison tattoos. I eventually got up the 42 stamps and was able to get four prison tats done with a homemade tattoo gun. You'll be surprised at the talent locked away in prisons.

I remained at the Beaumont prison for about two and a-half months, but was then relocated when all of the state's inmates were moved out of the facility and only the federal inmates kept. I was transferred to East Texas, to a prison called, the *Diboll Unit*, which was a level one/level two facility containing a little over 500 inmates. Here is where I would serve seven more months then be paroled due to good behavior.

At this prison, I was not on the kitchen crew, but was instead on the "Hoe Squad," which allowed inmates to work outside of the prison gates in the garden using garden tools just as a garden hoe, hence the name given, "Hoe Squad." Talk about the worse job on Planet Earth! First of all, this was Texas, and if you're from Texas or have been to Texas during the summer time, you know what the heat feels like, and it's beyond unbearable. Secondly, why would prison officials give convicted felons steel garden tools, which could easily be confiscated by an inmate and turned into a prison shank, and used as a weapon? Then on top of that, prison guards seemed like they were just ready to use their shotguns if somebody decided to make “a break for it” to attempt an escape.

A major fact of truth, or some quick game: when you get incarcerated it is imperative, if you desire to be released sooner than later, that you sign up for everything possible, go to work, keep a good record and focus on getting out!

I was not created to be a caged animal, so even though I did the crime, sittin’ behind four walls, fenced in by razor wire, and living with a mixture of inmates from all walks of life was not my type of living. So I choose to be focused on gettin' out, but only in the right way, even though my mind was not changed at this point. And that required me to participate on the "hoe squad".

It was at the Diboll unit that I began to learn the drug game. I went in mainly as a thief, but would come out with the head knowledge of movin' drugs, to which I added the practical aspect of sellin' when I hit the streets.

One of my closest friends that I was incarcerated with was an older "cat" that we called MIA since he was from Miami. He had served 6 years of fed time before but was now incarcerated in Texas for selling drugs in Texas.

He, I, and several others from various parts of Texas were pretty cool, as cool as you could get with people in prison. We would lift weights on the yard together, play basketball together, and talk extensively, him teaching me the game. MIA would tell me a lot about the drug game: how to condense drugs in cans, cocaine prices, possible connects, and so much more.

He had asked me once, or maybe several times, if I was interested in moving cocaine from Florida to North Carolina, where I would eventually be going after being paroled.

Since he was well connected with the Columbians and would get pure

Cocaine off the boats in Miami, he wanted to put me down with his organization to begin moving Coke up the East Coast. The plan was that when I got out, I would be "fronted" a "key" of Coke, and all I would have to do was bring him back $12,000 after the entire "key" was sold!

Cocaine is a quick money-making illegal hustle, where from one "key," a person can make $30,000 to $100,000 more or less rather easily depending on the cut, breakdown and clientele one has. The only problem was that I was scared to move Cocaine because of the amount of prison time a person could receive. Money has a way of manipulating situations, but I preferred moving

Marijuana than Cocaine, Heroin, or some of the other illegal drugs because of the lengthy time behind it.

Therefore, I informed M.I.A. that I wasn't interested in moving the Coke, but that I would move Marijuana instead, which I eventually did after I got out of prison, but not through his connects.

I came up for my first parole in July, 2002. After the parole hearing, I was not sure if I would be released or eventually sent to another prison, since the max a person would stay at Diboll was about two years. After about two months of waiting for an answer, I was called back to the parole hearing office to receive my answer. Talk about butterflies in the stomach! I was told that I was given an FI-2, which in Texas meant that I would be paroled in three months, but it did not specify the date on which I would be released.

Boy, was I happy!

But I made a big mistake: I told several people that I was gonna be released soon. Word to the wise, if you ever find yourself incarcerated, don't tell anyone when you are about to get out. Otherwise, you will see "close friends/associations" turn on you, as I did. People tend to get jealous instead of happy for you when they know that you're getting out and they would be staying in prison.

People started hating me and trying to instigate me to get into altercations with them, but my mind was on getting released and not worrying about what these guys would possibly do. I just had to continue to watch my back until I got released. As for MIA and a couple others, we continued to be cool. In fact, I kept up with MIA for a while when I had gotten released.

With the FI-2 all I had to do was ride out the three more months on my five-year sentence, stay out of trouble, and then I would be goin' home. It's easier said than done, but, praise the Lord, I was able to refrain from fighting, and beat the one case that I did end up catchin' a charge simply because a Corrections Officer had done some shady stuff, had wrote me up, but the Sergeant recognized it, so the charges were dropped on me. That was a relief!

Throughout my prison sentence, I had come into near fights but was able to avoid or de-escalate them. In prison I became tired of the fights that would go on and weary of missing holidays. I've missed everything on the calendar at least once, and some holidays I've missed twice or more, in fact. I was tired of the food, tired of being told when to eat, and tired of being told when to sleep and what to wear. Moreover, I was tired of having to look over my shoulder to avoid becoming a victim of prison rape—another sad reality of prison life.

I was in a level one/level two prison with guys that would eventually see the light of day, freedom, so there were not as many prison rapes as in level four and five prisons, where there are people with more violent crimes and who have a lot longer sentences, including lifers who have nothing to lose, nevertheless all manner of things went on!

Regardless of the prison's levels, I was beyond ready for my freedom!

The morning that I would be transferred back to Huntsville, Texas, to be processed, given a background check to make sure I didn't have any open warrants, and released finally came. I was picked up from the Diboll unit at 3:00 am, then the prison bus went to various prisons in Texas to pick up others, mainly people that were just coming into prison or were being transferred to other prisons; similar to how it was when I was first going to the Holliday Transfer Unit.

I remember sitting in the back of the *Blue Bird* prison bus, noticing a Caucasian male shackled behind a gate on the other side of the bus. He was talking with some others about his murder charge and various other things, but as I looked at him a feeling of fear came upon me. He was a young guy as well, but hard living made him look a little bit older than he actually was. As I glanced at his face, it was like evil radiated from his very being. He looked so evil that when I looked at him and he at me, it felt as if the devil was looking directly at me! I couldn't continue to look at this guy face-to-face, so I decided to look away. Indeed, I have seen some scary looking people in prison. People with all manner of tattoos on their bodies, some testifying to murders they have committed, to the gangs they rep and the things they stand for. People with tattoos on their faces, one of which I eventually got myself. People with the look of "I don't care" about anyone or anything in life, and in prison you are boxed in with people from every walk of life that you can think of. This can be an easy recipe for disaster.

December 18th, 2002 was the date I was finally released. We were taken to the Walls unit, which is a Death Row prison, where upon our release we were given $50 dollars, if you were a parolee, or $100 if you had maxed out on your sentence. The other $50 for a parolee would be given the next day when you would go to see your parole officer. We were then given our paperwork, let out, and then sent over to a Greyhound bus that would take now-free inmates to different cities in Texas to be picked up by family or others, if family was not at the Walls unit to pick them up.

My family wasn't present to pick me up, so I had to take the Greyhound to meet my oldest son's mother, who I would stay with for a couple of days. I had been incarcerated for thirteen months, starting November 19th, 2001 until December 18th, 2002.

I would remain in Texas for two weeks after being released and then transferred to North Carolina to finish out my three years and eleven months of parole. This move happened for several reasons, but the main reason that pervaded my mind was getting to N.C., establishing myself, then begin moving

Marijuana by the pound from Dallas, Texas to Southeastern North Carolina. It was time to get my "hustle on" in a new manner makin' some big money movin drugs!

But was I ready for the drama that comes with moving drugs in the "hood" on MLK where I wasn't from?

Terminology Defined

Chapter 15:

Hustla's-Someone that Knows How to

Make Money Multiple Types of Ways

Fire Green-Very Good Weed

Making my Name Hot-Known Around by

More People than You Want Knowing

Who You Are

Stick up Kids/Jack Boys-People Whose

Way of Making Money is by Robbing You

Get On-Be Able to Buy and Sell Product

Bounce Back-Make a Come Back after

Falling off

Flip It/Double Up-Make a Purchase then

Sell it, Make More Money then you Sold it

for, Come Back then buy More Product

then What you Bought the First Time

Weight-Amount of Drugs Selling

Re-Up-Get More Drugs

Take ya Lick-Accept Whatever Comes

Your Way

Chopper-AK-47 Assault Rifle

Chalk it to the Game-Let it Go

Chapter Fifteen

Moving Marijuana Through U.P.S.

I arrived in North Carolina January 10th, 2003. I was 20 years old. Since I had lived in North Carolina some years previously and had some distant cousins that lived there it wasn't a place that was completely foreign to me.

To begin establishing myself in the drug game in Southeastern North Carolina, I knew there were several people that I had to meet, and people I was already acquainted with and/or related to, knew those who I needed to connect with.

For a few months I was kind of at a dead end until I got up with one of my distant cousins who, like me, had a passion for making money, plus he had some good connections with people he had gone to high school with. Once we met up, he began to introduce me to various young "hustla's" around the town.

A little bit after meeting several guys, I began to set up things with my connect in Texas, planning to move the weed through the U.P.S. mailing system.

There are several ways to transport drugs across state lines, which are all risky, so we decided to go with what we felt was the least risky way of moving them, and that was through the mail.

If only the U.P.S. deliverers knew what they had in their boxes!

At times, some of the packages of weed would already be broken down into ounces and bagged up, but at other times the pound of weed would come all together of which I would break them down into ounces and smaller weights, then I would be ready to hit the block and let people know that I had some "fire" green for sale from Texas, and for less money than what almost everybody around the area charged.

My purpose was to sell each shipment that I received really fast. To do that, I would quickly hit the block when I had weed, getting rid of it in a matter of hours or within a day. In that way, I felt that the police wouldn't get wind of me, and I wouldn't have to be on the block making my name hot and hanging out on the corners with the other hustla's.

I sold dimes and nick bags, which were $10 and $5 bags of weed, respectively. They were the size of Texas dimes and nicks and were a lot fatter than the bags normally sold in North Carolina. Beyond that, the price that I was selling ounces for beat out most of the competition in the area. It was easy to get the weed off, but when hustlin', you always have to keep in mind that others have hustles as well so the problem is that you not only have to watch your back for the police, but also for "stick-up" kids and jack boys.

And I was about to get an experience at that!

It wasn't long before I had the practical side of hustlin' down pat, caring about the customer and how much weed they got in each bag and each ounce breakin' down marijuana perfectly, selling bags without stems and seeds, limiting the dusty shake of the weed, with all of my ounces weighing perfectly on the scale gram-wise. I was on my way to the top. I could get a pound of weed one day and be completely out of the package before the end of that day. That's how fast a pound of weed would sell at the rate I was going. But fate would take its toll, and I was about to be in a life-or-death situation.

Robbed for the Weed

My vision in the drug game was always, *"Why don't all of us who sell drugs in the hood work together as a team, uniting our prices, product, and surveillance against the police? That way, we can all get paid and be on one accord."* Unfortunately, no one seemed to catch my vision.

The drug game is really selfish, and on the streets it's "every man for himself," but that didn't keep me from selling weed at an affordable price. I would purposely sell my Marijuana at a price that would give everyone who wanted to "get on" the opportunity to be able to "get on", or if you just wanted to smoke and get high you could do that also.

For instance, I sold quarters or 7-grams of Marijuana for $15.00, while most of my competition sold them for $25.00-$30.00. Half ounces, or 14-grams, went for $30.00, while most of my competition sold them for about $60.00. I sold ounces, 28 grams, for between $50.00-$60.00, but most of my competition sold them for $75.00-$100.00. I was easily beating out the competition as far as prices were concerned, and this caused me to be able to move the product fast, make money fast, and to see others "get on". Plus, the price we were getting pounds for in Texas was a lot cheaper than what people were paying in North Carolina, allowing me to set my selling prices lower than the competition's.

In September of 2004, I was 21 years old, a month away from being 22. For almost a year, I had been on and off with selling Marijuana, learning more of the drug game step-by-step but would have times when I trusted people too much and would front stuff only to be played. On the streets, most of the time when you "front" something to somebody, especially drugs, you're not gonna get the money or the product back, but I had to learn this by trial and error. So, after falling off, I would bounce back by hustlin' on the street corner with the rest of the "cats," trying to build my "weight" back up. As soon as I started understanding the practical side of the drug game more fully getting into the swing of things forreal, getting' my weight back up, the robbery took place. What a coincidence!

Early that September morning, I had received a fresh pound of weed in the mail. As soon as I got the package, I began to break it down removing all the stems and seeds like normal. I bagged up ounces, half ounces, quarters, and some nicks and dime bags for those that just wanted to get high. The half ounces and quarters were mainly for those who wanted to purchase some weed to "flip it," "double up," and come back to get more weed to sell, as they were building up their clientele and "weight". That's the object of the drug game: flipping the product, building up clientele, and stackin' up a lot of money.

The plan that day was to sell as much weed as I could. Whatever I happened to not get off, I would stash in a hole that I would dig in the country, just in case the police were to raid my apartment. Close to evening, I had sold half of a pound and had another half remaining. From the first half pound that I had already sold that day I had made close to $500.00, which was done in a couple of hours. All I had to do was to get off the other half of a pound, which would generate a total of $1,000 in sales—all in less than 24 hours.

That's why "the game" is so addictive, because the money comes fast bringing a type of adrenaline rush that's rivaled by not much in life!

I ended up digging the hole that day, but after I had dug it, I decided that I wasn't going to put the weed in it. In the back of my mind, the thought was, "if a customer comes through and wants some weed, I want to serve him right then so that I could hurry up, get off the pound, and re-up." Had I put the weed in the hole, the robbery would not have taken place, at least not on that particular night.

Later that evening, after dark, several people came to my apartment buying nicks and dime bags from me, but then one guy, who I was cool with, came wanting to get half an ounce and another wanting to get the rest of the weed off me, which would be 7 ½ ounces. If I were to make this deal, I would be free of the entire pound, and then the next day I could send out the necessary money to get two pounds of weed in the mail for the next shipment. I could flip that and keep getting my weight and money up. The more pounds I could get, the faster the money would come.

The guy wanting the 7 ½ ounces was represented by a guy from the "hood" that I had done business with before. He asked me to come down the street to the park to make the transaction because he said too much traffic was coming through my apartment, so I felt he was lookin' out for me, trying to avoid possible police surveillance, of which my spot did in fact have a lot of traffic all that day.

Little did I know though that he was setting me up for a robbery. I decided to make the transaction in the park, which was a few hundred yards away from my apartment. Along with the middleman that helped set up the transaction, I drove down to the park and waited for the actual buyer to come.

After about five minutes, he showed up, walking down the street. When I saw him, I immediately said to myself, "I don't wanna mess with this guy." On the block, I had heard of him to be a jack boy and didn't want anything to do with him. I wanted to cancel the deal when I saw him, but the thought of selling this last little bit of weed I had left then heading to re-up was running all through my mind.

I decided to go through with the transaction, not knowing that I was about to be another one of his victims.

It's strange how money can influence a person to do some wild things!

When the guy reached my car, I got out, and we walked inside the park. He had his scale, a digital one, and I had mine, a finger scale. We first weighed out four ounces on his scale, but his scale seemed to be acting up, so I pulled out my finger scale, and we re-weighed each of the first four ounces, and all of them were coming to 28 grams to the tee. After we had weighed the four ounces, I said, "Show me the money for those four ounces." Then I would show him the rest of the weed, 3 and a half ounces, which I had in a book bag on my back. He immediately began digging in his pockets as if to show me the money for the first four ounces of weed. I watched him dig around in all four of his pockets, and as I was watching him, I knew that something bad was about to happen.

You see, on the streets when you're hustlin, people carry small bills, nothing larger than $20's, because you have to be able to make change for the customers and can't do that with bills like hundreds. The 7 ½ ounces was to sell for $450.00, so finding that in a big knot of money in his pocket should have only taken a few seconds. But as I watched him dig in each of his pockets, it seemed that time stopped and everything moved in slow motion.

At that point, I knew something bad was about to happen.

"Give me the rest of the weed homie," he demanded.

"Aight, dude, hol up. I got you."

Instead of pulling any money out of his pocket, he pulled out a .25 caliber pistol and put it a few inches away from my face. I hadn't seriously prayed in a long time, but at this point I decided to send up a quick prayer asking God to do whatever he was gonna do because I was in a life-or-death situation. Since I wasn't from the hood I was hustlin in, not havin' grown up with the dudes I was interacting with on a daily basis, not knowing these dudes for real, as well as the fact that my cousin who put me down with a lot of the guys on the block had moved away, left it so that I was essentially hustlin' solo, which was all a recipe for something bad to happen.

After I had given the jack boy the remaining 3 ½ ounces of weed that I had with me, he then told me to turn around. At this point, the gun was pointed at the back of my head. He told me to walk to my car, following me the entire time with the gun pointed at my head. He could have easily shot me and left me for dead—which happens very frequently on the streets. Though I was robbed, I was selling drugs, which is illegal, so I couldn't, nor wouldn't go tell the police what happened. Street rules is street rules and street justice takes place on a regular basis in hoods all across America. When you live by street codes, you just have to "take ya lick" and keep moving. This is the game!

After he had walked me to my car like a dog on a lease I had gotten into the car and the dude with the gun had stepped back. I immediately cranked up my car and leaned my seat as far back as it could possibly go, so that if he fired at the car, the bullets would go over my head instead of in my head and through the window. As I was speeding off, I heard him fire the gun. Whether or not he fired the gun in the air or at me, I don't know.

Whether or not he was trying to pull the trigger while he had it at the back of my head, I don't know. What I do know though, is that despite the fact that I wasn't living a life for God at this point, my life was spared!

Minutes after the robbery, I went back to my apartment. I knew that I had been set up because the guy who came to my apartment to arrange the deal had told me that another person wanted to buy the weed. But the person that robbed me was not the person that was originally named. Had I known that the guy who robbed me was the one who wanted the weed from the beginning, I wouldn't have agreed to attempt to make that drug sale.

Just a few weeks after this event took place, a young guy who I was familiar with was shot in the head and killed over $5.00 dollars' worth of weed in the same hood in which I was robbed. Hundreds of dollars of weed were taken from me, but this guy was killed over $5.00 worth of Marijuana! Bullets don't care about a number; they only do what the person holding the gun does. The streets are dangerous, and it's no place for anyone to be who values his freedom and life. Not everyone who goes out into the "world" or who is even born and raised in these types of environments are able to make it back with his or her life or with his or her freedom or even survive through it all for that matter.

Word spread fast in the hood about what happened to me that night. Early that next morning, several guys were at my house trying to get me to buy a bulletproof vest, choppers, and sawed-off shotguns. It felt like it was about to be a war zone, but after the robbery took place, I called several people, and they advised me to forget what happened and "chalk it to the game," as the expression goes. My brother, a movie fan, said, "Life is not a movie; it's reality. If you die in this life, you don't come back to star in the next role!"

That hit me and hit me hard!

"Life is not a movie". There was so much truth to that statement. In the movies, we see people get killed, but it's only a movie, and not reality. Living this life, however, is reality. And if a person gets killed out here on these streets, then that's it! One more son or daughter lost, one more father or mother lost, one more cousin or aunt or uncle lost. One more friend lost to the streets. The circle of violence continues.

I refused to retaliate. I was no killer, and I was no thug, and I never claimed to be some hardened street cat. I had a passion for fast money, not for killing, and was not ready to take it to that level of a warzone. When I look back, I'm thankful that I wasn't high on Ecstasy or drinking alcohol or on Coke when the robbery occurred. Had I been, the drugs would have taken over, and I probably would have reacted in a manner that could have cost me my life or freedom.

I let it go!

It was hard to do, because each day on the block, I would see the guy who robbed me, and with that it's easy for most people to assume that I was a coward. But I tell you this, while I'm not a coward, I'm glad that I had people who advised me properly because I could have easily been dead right now or locked up for the rest of my life. Have I done dumb things with guns before, yes, but I didn't want an all-out street war over only a half a pound of weed! It wasn't worth it in my opinion! So, I let it go!

The streets have codes, "kill or be killed", "no snitchin'", "get it how you live," and many more, but I tell you, so often it's simply everyone for him or herself and you gotta think for yourself, being analytical to things goin' on around you. If you kill somebody out there, you do the time by yourself, and your "friends" are often nowhere to be found. No letters, no visits, no phone calls—nothing! If you get killed out there, it's you that ceases to exist while life goes on. Be your own person, never let others manipulate you into something you know isn't right to do. Also, always have people around you who give you wisdom as to moves you should and shouldn't make. It will make a world of difference.

I'd like to say that after that experience I changed my life and I started following God. But that didn't happen, and it would still be another four years before I would give my life to God.

Terminology Defined

Chapter 16:

Sucker for Love-Somebody that Looks for Love

Gift of Gab-Ability to Talk Smooth to Get What You Want

Chick-Female

Go Both Way's-Bi-Sexual

O.E.-Olde English, a Type of Malt Liquor

Pimping-People into Manipulating People for Services

Mash Out-To Go Somewhere

Dressed Fly-The Clothes Look Good

Fire-Nice Looking

Chapter Sixteen

Girls, Girls, Girls!

"I'm pregnant, I'm pregnant, I'm pregnant, I'm pregnant, I'm pregnant, I'm pregnant, I'm pregnant, I'm pregnant", in between my incarcerations, drug use, drug selling, making and losing money; women, sexual relationships and pregnancies have continuously been a theme from my young teenage years onward.

Sadly, I can't tell you the first female that I had sex with! In fact, I can't tell you many of the women's names that I have had sexual intercourse and relations with. In my heart of hearts, I've always only been interested in being with one woman and growing old with that one particular person. Call me a sucker for love, I can accept that, however, because I tended to look up to friends, getting advice from people who I thought knew the "game", I became a person that learned how to use, manipulate and "play" women for whatever I wanted.

Gift of Gab

"Say my dude, peep, it's this chick at work that go both ways", I had told my homeboy. At the time I was workin' at a McDonald's near Ft. Worth, Texas, and on this particular day I was assigned to work the drive thru takin' orders.

One of my managers, who was in her mid-twenties, several years older than myself, and some months before I had gone to prison, mistakenly blurted out on the drive thru headset to where I could overhear, “the girl in the car is sexy.” In my mind, that was a cue that let me know what this girl (my manager) was about.

After she said what she had said, I approached her while we were still at work to confirm audibly what I already was aware of internally. “Peep, what’s good, I know you like women and I hear you talkin’ bout men as well, I’m tryin’ to see what's up”, as the conversation ensued between my manager and I, realizing and relishing in the fact that she goes both ways, I was excited! She gave me her number, and at that point, I knew I was all in!

Within a few days of connectin' with her outside of work I had manipulated her to the extent that she was buying me my daily alcohol, which was mainly 40 oz bottles of O.E. and packs of cigarettes, Newport Shorts in a box, of which I was smokin' a pack a day. In addition, it was only a matter of days before I was at her house havin' sexual relations with her. True to form though, like the old street loyalist adage goes, "ain't no fun if the homies can't have none", rang true for me as well. After my first encounter with her, I let some of my friends know about the situation and was able to get them onboard.

Once I had orchestrated things between this young lady, myself and about 3 of my homeboys to be able to all meet up at her house, everything else as they say, was history.

I was 18 years old at the time, but had learned how to manipulate situations with women, to where I would use women, made in the image of God, for sex, to get money out of, to do things for me that they may have never thought to do prior to encountering me; all for my personal pleasure and gratification!

The manipulation, in my mind, was to a level where I had considered pimpin' females and/or club promoting and being responsible for gettin' the girls. While I never got involved in pimpin' women, the thought had lingered in my mind on and off for some years.

The Night Life

"Say fool (term of endearment in Texas), let's hit up the strip club." This is something that would be heard coming out of my mouth on a frequent basis. While I was living in Dallas, Texas or Baton Rouge, Louisiana, my homies and I would get our narcotics, grab the gun that we kept fully loaded at all times, hop in the car and mash out to the strip club.

By the time we would get to the club we would have consumed some Cocaine, some Ecstasy pills and would be tipsy off the alcohol. Nevertheless, we needed to celebrate makin' it through yet another week of hard livin', drug usage, frustrations, hustlin', workin' legit jobs and/or just tryin' to keep our heads above water.

"How much it cost to get in?" I ask the bouncer at the front door of the club. "$10.00", came back the reply. After we each pay our money to get in, we make our way to the bar, already tipsy off the alcohol, high off the Coke and pills, but still needing more intoxicants to vibe with the flow inside of the club.

Lights down low, music beatin' loud and heavy, feelin' the vibrations in our very souls, seein' the women gyrating as the DJ keeps things flowin' in full swing. Girls on the stage workin' the polls, some there tryin' to pay their way through college, others there tryin' to feed their kids and others there simply tryin' to have a quick hustle and come up! Regardless, the atmosphere was my type of thing; relaxed and chilled with visual pleasure to stimulate my very being!

After gettin' a drink from the bar I head over to the stage for a close-up view of the women. I'm dressed fly in my fresh white T, some clean and crisp jeans on, a fitted hat and some fire Reebox Classics on my feet. I'm ready for the night! After standin' by the stage for a bit, I then walk over to an empty seat. Now it's time for me to sit down and watch the young ladies work their magic from the comfort of a soft chair as if I'm at the movie theater, only this is live and direct! "Would you like a lap dance?" A young lady asked in a soft delicate voice with a passionate smile, my reply, "Naw, I'm good, just lookin'." You see, the only thing I was payin' for was to get in the strip club, because I wasn't into given women money for anything, let alone a lap dance, that I could get from a female elsewhere for free. This was my philosophy, not really respecting the hustle of the ladies on stage or women in general, which would lead me to be selfish in many ways.

Being in the strip club for several hours, well into the early morning, we would stay till closing time which was around 2am then be done for the night. We would then leave, probably stoppin' at a fast-food restaurant to get somethin' to eat or a waffle house where various parking lot parties would be transpiring. Bein' that we had drank as much alcohol as we had, snorted a good amount of Cocaine, and popped pills, we needed to feed our bodies with food before headin' in for the night.

This was a common weekend for us!

The women, the allure of the night life, the drugs and drinking, the disrespect for a women's body, I was, in hindsight, one of the lowest types of people in the world, one who used many women for their bodies and money!

But change was soon to come on every level; My running from God couldn't stand to hold up much longer.

Chapter Seventeen

(That) Beginning of the End

The sellin' of drugs had ceased but during the last six months of my runnin' from God, I immersed myself heavily in drug usage, tryin' to OD while simultaneously tryin' to "fry" the Holy Spirit out of my mind! Tired and frustrated, I wanted to be done with life and finished with hearing God's voice trying to get my attention. Although I had a .38 caliber pistol, I had no interest in taking the messy way out by shooting myself in the head. So, what better way than to consume so many drugs at one time that I would simply die in my sleep never again to wake up from the high?!

No More Running (Chapter 1 Revisited)

On **Sunday, April 6th, 2008**, in the city of B.R., short for Baton Rouge, Louisiana, I began my day as I normally liked, a little breakfast to hold the alcohol. Then it was time to begin my intoxicants. Starting with beer, I downed thirteen 12-ounce cans of *Bud Light*, then I snorted a $20 bag of Cocaine that I had gotten from the rapper Lil' Boosie's neighborhood on BR's South Side, and I smoked some weed with a co-worker of mine. How was I able to function throughout the day? Simple answer. I had built up such a high tolerance for drugs and alcohol from steadily taking them since I was 15 that at 25, though I had a small frame and only weighed 150 pounds, I could "handle my alcohol", as the saying goes.

Monday, April 7th, 2008, was no exception. You see, I was not just a weekend drug user; this was an everyday event, a seven-days-a-week habit that I was driven to fulfill.

That day I had enough money to buy a double-stack Ecstasy pill that I popped, but I later found it was mixed with too much "speed," which caused me not to sleep properly for the next two days. Through it all, I didn't see that God was silently at work, ordering events in my life in several ways.

Wednesday, April 9th, 2008,

rolled around. It was the day that was to forever change my life. Like other days, this day was no exception to my rule. I snorted a dime bag of Cocaine, although I knew the chemicals from the powder constantly corroded my nostrils, causing frequent nosebleeds. Yeah, I knew that the things I was doin' had harmful effects on mc, but at the time I did all these drugs, my only thought was relief from reality and the fun of being high, which drowned out all thoughts of the drugs' negative effects.

As the day continued, I drank a 24-ounce can of *Bud Light* Beer and smoked some weed with my next-door neighbor, while at the same time standing outside playin' around with a .22 Caliber rifle. However, the high from Monday's Ecstasy pill had not completely worn off; it was still in my bloodstream and affected my mind and body, keeping me from being able to sleep for the last few days.

I hadn't slept since Sunday night, which was normal because of the large amount of drug "uppers" that I consumed.

On the brink of self-destruction that Wednesday, I came inside the house at 11:30pm feelin' good from the high and doin' what I do!

After coming into the house, I then went into my room, never to come out the same person again! As I was walking into the room, I stopped and stood in the doorway for a few seconds because I could immediately sense that there was an evil presence in the room! As I continued to go into the room, a fear came upon me like never before! This was nothing like any Cocaine "spook" that I had experienced before. I could literally feel that something evil was in the room. After I closed the blinds, partly because of paranoia from the effects of the Marijuana and Cocaine, I laid down, "high as a kite," on my mattress and looked up at the ceiling. Boy, was I not ready to see what was happening there! My eyes seemed to be "opened" at that point, and I actually saw demons floating around on the ceiling wall. It was something like out of *Indiana Jones and the Raiders of the Lost Ark*, when at the end of the movie the "Ark of the Covenant" had been opened and demons began to weave in and out of people. It was a scary sight to behold, one that I will never forget!

What was happening in that room that night, I did not want to see! Like a little child I took the cover and pulled it over my eyes. The spiritual world seemed to be revealing itself to me, that veil that separates humanity and the spiritual realm was being pulled back. At that point

I heard a voice, just as audible as someone speaking to me, but it was the voice of the Holy Spirit, and he said something that I will never forget, calling me by name!

As clear as day, the Holy Spirit said, *"Aaron, either you get your life together now, or that's it!"*

Those very words frightened me to the very core of my bones! Why? Because I knew what the unpardonable sin is. I had grown up in the church and had a good understanding of what was going on at that point; I knew that the frightening words *"Let him alone, Ephraim is joined to his idols"* was about to happen to me. I was on the brink of committing the unpardonable sin, the only sin that God cannot forgive!

You see, for years I had been running from the Lord, and for the last 6-months, as I stated earlier, I was on a mission to "fry" the Holy Spirit out of my conscience. Every time I would hear the Holy Spirit trying to get my attention, I would purposely get "high" on coke, weed, Ex-Pills, prescription pills, alcohol, or possibly some heroin, so that I could tune Him out.

What in the world was I doing?

On that fateful Wednesday night, my eyes were so much more opened to the fact that I had been placing myself on dangerous ground, and Satan was about to be allowed full control over my life!

After the Holy Spirit spoke to me, I knew that I had to do something. I was trying to think of whom I could call. I thought of my ex-wife, but I knew that she didn't want to hear anything from me, especially since our divorce papers had just come through. If I would have called any of my homeboys, they would have given me the common prescription that most friends that drink and do drugs would have said: "Drink a beer, smoke a blunt, go to sleep, then call me in the morning. Doctor's orders!" I knew I didn't need to hear that, so the only other person that I could think of calling was my dad.

At the time he was in Georgia while I was in Baton Rouge, Louisiana, which meant there was an hour's difference between us; so, it was almost 1:00am where he was, and I knew that he would be asleep, but I had to throw out a lifeline to someone, hoping it would be grabbed, like a fish on a hook, because I was on the verge of eternal destruction. I grabbed my cell phone and texted these very words, *"I feel lost and friendless."*

After I sent the text message, I had no clue what was gonna happen next. Five minutes had passed then my phone lit up with a response from my father. It stated these very words, *"What a friend we have in Jesus."* Boy, was I happy to get that text! Immediately, I got on the phone and called my dad. We talked for about ten to fifteen minutes, and I poured my heart out to him, asking, "How can you and Mom be so content with having no money, yet do full-time ministry work? And why am I so miserable—through all of the things that I had done in life, yet still no real joy?" Before we finished talking, my dad stated that he would come out to Baton Rouge that coming Friday and pick me up. He advised me not to go to work the next day, where I worked for a lube shop changing oil on cars, because he said that Satan would make sure that I forgot all about what happened the previous night. So, I made the decision that I would not go to work and I would wait for him to come get me. After talking, we prayed together.

Right after that, I got on my knees once again and began to pray for myself. It's always good for someone to be praying for you. No doubt you've heard of people saying that they would not be around "if it wasn't for a praying grandmother." Well, for me it was praying parents, but even though someone prays for you, you still at some point need to pray for yourself. That's what I did that night. As I was on my knees praying to God, I could literally feel Satan and the weight of the world, in Jesus' name, rising off my back. This was a great feeling! One that everyone who's running from God can also experience! After I finished praying, I grabbed the Christian book *The Great Controversy*, which so happened to be in my possession, and turned to chapter 32, "Snares of Satan". I knew that the devil was about to be on the prowl, and I had to begin reading to understand some of his tactics and filling my mind with spiritual things.

The next day, even in a daze from the previous night's events, I continued reading Christian books like *Steps to Christ* and *Patriarchs and Prophets.*

My dad arrived in BR to pick me up by mid-Friday morning **April 10th, 2008**, having begun my journey to the cross just hours earlier.

I'm not gonna lie and say it was easy, because it wasn't by any means. For two months, I battled to overcome the drugs, alcohol, and nicotine addictions that I had, but one thing was for sure: I was determined to get on track! As I continued to come to the cross, I read the Word of God every morning, one chapter at a time, no matter what I would do during the day. As I continued doing this, I began to see that the Lord was cleaning me up. I came as I was, and I was allowing

Jesus to change me instead of trying to change myself then coming to Jesus.

By **June 8th, 2008** God had taken all of those tastes away from me and now as you read this book, it has been over 15 years since I have used any drugs or drank any alcohol!

I finally came to the end of my running from God, and it finally felt good and a right time to stop!

JailLyfe: Jesus Always Is Looking

Chapter Eighteen

Everybody Doesn't Make It Back: With Their Life or With Their Freedom

Perhaps in your life, no matter your age, the thought of, "I'm tired of church and would like to experience the world", may have run through your mind. If you have ever felt this way or have thought this exact thought, I want you to consider the statement, *"Everybody doesn't make it back, with his or her life or with his or her freedom."*

I want to introduce you to a couple people who grew up as Seventh-day Adventist Christians, who even at some point went to Seventh-day Adventist Church Schools, but who still fell victim to the streets, one of whom was executed by lethal injection December 2020.

Also, I would like to introduce you to a person who grew up in a Christian home, but is not here to tell his story.

Our first person was forty years old when he was executed. His name is Brandon Bernard, and here's his testimony, written in 2011 for this book, when he was thirty-one:

I'm a grown man sitting on Federal Death Row. Twelve years of my life (22 years incarcerated at the time of his execution) are gone. Since the age of eighteen, I have called concrete walls, electric doors, and handcuffs my home.

What hurts most as I lay on my thin narrow mattress, staring at the ceiling at night, is that this could've been avoided as easy as stepping around a quarter size puddle on an empty four lane highway. I could have done something better with myself. I knew the winning numbers of the lottery, but I still wanted to try someone else's ticket.

Now I find myself in a place where there is mentally no peace. No contentment. Sometimes, I feel as though one thing will make everything better, but as soon as I think the hole is filled, another takes its place. Outside of God and doing what is right, there is never any true peace.

The Bible says, “The wages of sin is death”. When I embraced what I knew was contrary to what I was taught as a Seventh-day Adventist, I essentially turned in my application to the devil. I had an arrogance that came with my youthfulness, and it masked my ignorance of my future. I was fixated on the here and now. For an immediate good time, I was willing to throw away my whole life.

I was a young man employed by the devil. Now, every day I wake up in this cold box; I’m living off the pension plan in which I invested. I wanted it all. I wanted to have a life of fun. I wanted money. I wanted ladies in my bed. I wanted the respect of my circle. But I wanted it all for free. At least what I thought was free, but a heavy tab was stored for later. I ultimately got what I wanted for a little bit of time, and then got what I deserved for a lifetime.

I tried to balance two worlds, my Christian friends and lifestyle and the streets. Two worlds that don't match at all! When I wasn't running around in the streets, I thought I was missing something. I saw how my friends were acting, and it looked fun from the outside, but it was and still is all false. Once I found myself engrossed in the lifestyle I coveted so much, I saw how unglamorous things really were.

A hatred and disdain for life and others grew in my heart. I knew if I continued on the road I had chosen, I would be either dead or in prison, where street life always ends. I had to always look over my shoulder. Everyone I thought was my friends ended up betraying me. It is the same story for everyone before me and after me. Everyone on my prison tier could tell you the same story.

We all knew the end game. We were all told, but didn't listen. In the back of my head I thought, "Not me. Not *me*. I won't be in that situation!" But yes, it happened to me, and it can happen to you. See, therein lies the deception the devil imposes on his employees. Even though my lifestyle of sin was worse than my lifestyle of righteousness, I still stayed in it, as many of you reading this may choose to do. But know this: it will never change; you will end up dead or in prison for the rest of your life if you continue in the streets.

That's a fact!

Another reason that I strayed was that I thought there was a sacrifice of fun involved if I were to remain a young man of God. I thought I had to choose between having fun as a sinner or being bored as a Christian. The Bible says, "Choose," meaning you cannot have both worlds. Either you are one or the other, but being a real Christian is in no way boring.

I wish I would have understood that back in 1998 before I ended up in this situation. I wish I would have found joy in what I was doing, instead of reaching for what I didn't need. "There's a way that seemeth right unto a man, but the end thereof is death."

I had great times with my friends and family in Christ. However, like so many young people, I was so distracted by the devil that I never appreciated or even noticed the good times. I was selling myself short. I was eating the seeds and spitting out the watermelon, which is totally backwards.

Don't end up like me, thinking you always have tomorrow to get right. Take it from me.... One day, tomorrow doesn't come. Act now, because hell can find a home on earth.

(Brandon Bernard was executed by Lethal Injection at the Terre Haute, Indiana Federal Penitentiary on December 10th, 2020 with myself as his childhood friend and personal Pastor (Minister of Record) by his side in the Death Chamber as he took his last breaths on this earth)!

Our second person is Prescott Smith from New Orleans, Louisiana. Here's his story:

When I was a kid, my godmother used to bring me to church with her, and by the time I was seven, I had been baptized. Church became a second home for me, mainly because I had made a lot of friends there, as opposed to the loner that I was while at home. Church gave me something to always look forward to. Even though I had accepted Christ as my personal Savior, followed the Ten Commandments, kept the Sabbath, ate only the things that Adventist eat and was overall a good kid, there was something still missing from my life, and that was a personal intimate, love relationship with God.

Without having that solid foundation with God at the center, my life began to take a turn for the worse. By the time I was thirteen, I had seen almost everything that the mean streets of New Orleans had to offer. To see a kid commit a crime in my neighborhood was just as normal as seeing a kid ride a bike. During the summer, after my 9th grade year at Ephesus Junior Academy, my sister had gotten arrested by the F.B.I. Fearing that I would get arrested also, my mom and godmother sent me to an Adventist Boarding School in South Texas where some friends of mine from New Orleans were.

After about six months in Texas, I had gotten expelled from school for sneaking into the girl's dorm. I really didn't need any money at school because the school took care of all my needs, but I had fallen in love with money before I left New Orleans, and now, having been expelled, I was headed back home to a life of poverty.

When I made it home, my love for money, which had been asleep in Texas, awakened. Seeing that my mom had bills to pay and I needed clothes, shoes, and a car, I decided to start selling drugs. Selling them was easy. I knew a lot of people who sold and used Crack, making it easily my drug of choice to sell. My mother gave me $100, and I took half of it to invest in buying drugs. I began to make money instantly.

Eventually, I stopped going to church and began hanging on the block all the time. School, however, was very important to me, so I continued to attend, but I sold Crack the entire time I was there. Being involved in the drug trade and committing a host of other crimes didn't stop me from graduating. I was the only one of my mother's children to graduate, and it really made her proud.

After graduation I decided to go to college. I enrolled at Delgado Community

College, and at the end of my first semester I had a 3.06 grade point average. I really enjoyed school, but at the beginning of my second semester I was arrested for Armed Robbery and Attempted Kidnapping. My whole world was crushed!

Being locked up made me pray more often and more sincerely, which helped me build a real relationship with God for the first time in my life. God became real to me. We would communicate with one another. He wasn't a concept like before. Even though I was walking the walk, I still struggled with entertaining sinful thoughts running through my mind. I had spent almost ten months in jail before I copped out to a five-year probation deal. It would be a good thing to say that I had learned my lesson, but that wouldn't be the truth.

After only a month on the streets, I started drugs again, and I became more violent and more dangerous. Around this time, I felt as though the world owed me something. I gained a lot of respect on the streets, and many people knew my name. I knew what I was doing was wrong, but somehow it felt so good. The worst part of it all was that I had forgotten about God.

Seventeen months later, I was arrested again for Armed Robbery and a Second-Degree Kidnapping Charge. I spent almost two years in jail fighting the charges. My only son was born during this time, and he has never known me as a free man since he was born. That hurts a lot! My decisions not only affected me, but they also continue to affect my family and friends even today. For the new charges, I was not given probation or a second chance this time; I was found guilty and sentenced to 198 years in the infamous Angola State Penitentiary in Louisiana.

For the last ten years, give or take some (Now 24/25 years at time of publishing), I have been an inmate in Louisiana. The reality is that I could die here—all because of bad choices and my inner lust for fast money and the streets. The street life may appear glamorous, but it always ends in two ways, death or prison. I know that is the same song that you have heard preached for years, but the fact of the matter is that it's true. The street game provides no retirement plan, no future, and no hope. Just instant gratification, which eventually fades away, like a puff of white smoke into the thin air.

God has a plan for all of us, but it is our duty to find out what that plan is. If we listen, watch, and wait for Him, He will reveal His plan to us. If we become distracted, as in my case and so many others like mine, then we are like the Seed that fell among thorns. We allow the cares of riches and pleasures of this life to choke us to eternal death. This causes us to have no fruit, and it hinders us from carrying out the plan that God has for our lives.

Our third person, Joshua Andre Williams is not living to be able to tell his story. He was murdered at 20 years old. His mother, Kathleen Hill, writes these words to you:

An unplanned pregnancy led me to have Joshua Andre Williams! Giving birth was painful but at the same time a moment too difficult to describe; mixed emotions I felt! Looking down and holding my baby boy for the first time felt unreal. A new person that I was responsible for was connected to me. I felt different, I was a mother. I was in love with this baby boy and I felt that this little fellow loved me. Bringing him home brought so much excitement to my mother's house. Just as I had fallen in love with Josh my mother had fallen in love with him as well. So much attention he received, he was the first child, first grandchild, and first nephew. Josh was a good baby, only cried when hungry and wet. Sometimes he would cry to be put down, he never liked to be held for a long time. He smiled all the time with one dimple showing. People often told me he looked exactly like Martin Lawrence and Alex Pruitt off of “Home Alone”.

Josh appeared to be a quiet child but was very comical and sneaky. Growing up he made straight A’ and B’s in school. He played football and loved to go to the Chris Wilcox (Former NBA Player) basketball camp during the summer. On weekends he used to spend time with his father who stayed in South Carolina at the time and would go during the summer as well. In 2003 while Josh was in middle school, he experienced the loss of his father due to a car accident. Joseph Andre Williams died on impact. Josh was quiet when he was informed of what happened. Josh stared at his father while he was lying in the morgue. He never said a word. At the funeral, Josh showed no emotions. Months after losing his father he started playing recreational football. One Saturday morning during a game, he made his first touchdown and I was so happy that I was screaming, "Go Josh Go"! I was very excited. I looked at him and he had tears rolling down his cheeks and I asked him what was wrong and his response was "My daddy is not here to see me" and started crying even more. That moment was very unexpected of him showing emotions of the loss of his father. All I could do is tell him that things will get better and it will be alright. Not realizing then, that losing a loved one would ever be alright.

The older Josh became the more he talked about his father. Older people would call him Lil' Dre being that he looked so much like his father. Josh started calling himself Lil' Dre as well. At the age of 16 he started working with a youth program YWCA doing janitorial work at the Elementary School. There he worked with 3 grown men and they all bragged on how his work ethic was good. Josh was loved by many people. Moving from the small town of Whiteville, NC to a smaller town just a few miles away, Chadbourn, wasn't hard for him to make friends. These were two rivalry towns that went at it even when my mother was a little girl. Josh would hang around boys from each town that often fought each other but never in the presence of Josh. He was a very likeable young man. I would always tell him that I didn't want any mess at my house and he would tell me "Ma, I'm cool with all of them and they know I don't play". I would laugh and tell him to sit his small tail down. Never a dull or quiet moment when Josh was in the room. His imitation of Martin Lawrence would have you laughing extremely hard! He had Martin and just about all his episodes down to the tee. One day him and his siblings were playing church in the living room and Josh was the preacher. He had the bible and told us to turn to the book of Jonah. He gave a few points on the chapters and ended it with a topic that was "You can run but you can't hide". He knew that was him!

Josh started hanging out more in the streets with his friends and started smoking weed. I found this out because I had a recorder on my house phone being that I worked at night. He thought God was showing me what he was doing. His grades started dropping and he didn't have enough credits to pass his grade. He refused to dress out for JROTC so in that subject he flunked. That year I talked and talked to him but nothing changed. In spite of the change I was seeing in my son not one time did he disrespect me. I gave him 6 months to bring his grades up or I was going to send him off to Job Corp.

After the 6 months, things were still the same yet now progressed and were getting worse. He didn't agree to my decision and stated he didn't want to stay with me anymore so he moved out with my sister back to Whiteville, NC, from where we had moved previously. I had to sign papers stating that my sister was his guardian in order for him to get in school there. I didn't want to do it but if it took that to help him, I was willing. He couldn't get in regular school so he had to go to the academy. Josh became an A/B student again but refused to go back the following school year.

I then started hearing rumors and accusations of him being involved in break-ins but nothing was concrete. Finally, he made the decision to do what I encouraged him to do from the start and that was to attend Job Corps. He stayed there a little over a month and came home for the holiday and never went back. During this time more and more rumors were going around about him. One guy accused him of being involved with his trailer burning down but still that was a rumor. Josh decided to move to Newark, New Jersey with his father's mother. He stayed there for about 2 months and got sick and was hospitalized for a few days. I never knew what really happened. His grandmother seems to think he was given something that was too strong for him. I went to Jersey to see him with the possibility of bringing him back. While in the hospital he kept stating he had to get it right. I know right from wrong he stated. "I'm a running prophet and the Lord is dealing with me", he stated. He knew the Lord had something else in store for him and the streets wasn't it. He came back home with me. While away, there was a warrant issued for his arrest. Cops were looking at him and at a couple of residents. Rumors increased and I became scared for my son. I had heard he was involved in stealing copper from a man's house, Josh not knowing though that the man was watching them, also the man had a gun and could have shot them if he wanted to. Many days and nights I cried. I prayed and fasted for my son. I knew this wasn't the plan of the Lord. I would pray that his friends would be scattered and for the Lord to arrest his mind spiritually. I made the decision that the next time the cops would call or contact me I would help them find him. It hurt, but I said to myself that I'd rather see him locked up and behind bars than in a casket. Others didn't agree but it wasn't about them and I remember my prayer. I asked the Lord to arrest him spiritually and by me covering up and telling the cops I don't know where he is, that would be going against what I wanted the Lord to do. The next call came and I informed them of his whereabouts, it crushed me but I knew it would save him. I knew he was safe. He ended up going to jail but got out in a few months. I remember my pastor telling me one night in bible study that the Lord hears my prayers and for me to not worry about Josh because He had him. She even told me that Josh was going to go back to jail again but this time the Lord was really going to deal with him and this time there would be a change. She said that even the last time he was locked up the Lord was speaking to him. As a mother, who wants to hear that their child is going back to jail? I didn't, but just shook my head because I believed that the Lord speaks through her.

He did go back to jail and this time he spent 9 months there. I couldn't understand the length of time being that some charges were dropped and his lawyer would have me thinking he had time served but was just waiting on a signature on his paperwork to get released. The next time we were thinking he was going to get out, either somebody went on vacation or was sick so he didn't get released when he was expecting to. I realized then that this had to be God allowing this to happen in order to work on Josh some more.

While in jail Josh's conversation during his visits and over the phone sounded different, he talked about how he was tired and ready to give up on the streets. He often said "Ma, I see what it is, nobody cares about you when you get locked up."

November 2011 Josh had finally gotten out of jail. I was glad to receive the phone call "Ma come pick me up" and without any hesitation I was there. He was outside waiting on me, all I could see is that one dimple with a big smile on his face. He got in the car and I remember smelling cigarette smoke and said "boy you already started smoking" he said, "Ma do you know how long I went without a cigarette?" He had told me that by the time he walked out the door a man was in a truck smoking a cigarette and Josh had asked for one. He began to tell me how some people are going to be mad at him because he was choosing to be done with them. Josh stayed at my house until he got mad with one of my friends that I had checking on my house while I was out of town during the Thanksgiving Holiday. She told him that he couldn't have his girlfriend staying at his mama's house. He left and went to a family member's house; from there he would go wherever he and his girlfriend could go together.

The majority of his time was spent around her. He always stayed in contact and would come by and stay a day or two and leave. He would often call for a plate of food. I wasn't too worried about him, especially being that he was talking differently than he had been before. My neighbor informed me that when I was out of town, he cut Josh's hair and he was shocked by the words that were coming out of Josh's mouth. He stated that Josh was telling him that he doesn't do anything anymore and how people still look at him as the "old Josh" but he is nothing like the old person anymore. Josh would often tell me "Ma, I changed, you feel me…" He started calling me all day and night off and on, sometimes 3 and 4 o'clock in the morning just to talk and I remember him calling me sometimes at those times of the morning and saying "never mind", I said "okay" and went back to sleep. I remember when the new year came in 2012 and he called me around 12:30am asking me if I was just getting out of church and he said that he was calling to tell me "Happy New Year" and of course I said it back to him and we said we love each other and got off the phone. My phone rang about 3 more times back-to-back and it was him. I remember asking him if he thought something was going to happen to me and he said "no, Ma I'm just calling to make sure you are okay." Josh changed so much and emphasized to me how much he loved me that, I began to feel like it was my time to leave this world.

On 1-3-12 I visited him in the apartment complex the same one he got shot in. He came outside and sat in my car. We talked for a little over an hour. He began to tell me "Ma, I don't do anything. All I do is chill; I'm not going to lie I smoke a little weed here and there but that's it. You feel me Ma, I chill with my girl." I got my hug from him and an, "I love you" and went to work.

On 1-8-12 I received a tap on my shoulder in church and looked and it was my son Josh asking me if he could sit down on my row, and of course I made room for him and his girl to sit. During the service I remember looking at him asking him not to leave being that he would often come to church but sit in the back and when I would turn around looking for him, he would be gone just as quick as he had come. It wasn't very usual for him to sit in front with me but it made me feel good that he did this day. After asking him not to leave, his response was, "Ma, I'm not going anywhere." He remained at church the entire service. I walked him outside, he then smiled and said "ma you know I don't have a dime in my pocket but I'm happy, you feel me, I'm happy…we hugged and said our "I love you's" then I went home to finish cooking before going back to work.

My phone rang and I told myself I would call him once I got back in the van due to me trying to rush and finish cooking. I got the van on my way to work and the phone rang again and it was Josh asking me what I had cooked. I told him and he stated that he was hungry, I then told him that I was on my way to work but I would call someone to make sure he had something to eat. He said “okay” and got off the phone.

I got to work and was talking to my co-worker when the phone rang again but this time it was my sister telling me he got shot. I was like no, I just talked to him, I just got off the phone with him and she said you need to come to the hospital. I remember my co-worker grabbing me telling me to calm down and not to drive. I got in my car and all I could say is how and what happened? A 15-minute drive took forever. Pulling up to the ER seeing cars and people, my heart fell. Getting out of the car, people began coming up to me left and right asking me if I'm okay and I'm thinking I don't know anything. I went straight to the window and asked the receptionist if I could go in the back of which she stated he was in surgery. His girlfriend walked up to me telling me what happened and I'm like the story didn't sound right but it wasn't time for that then she began to tell me that they put him in the car and brought him to the ER and he told them that he loved them and for them to tell me he loved me. I remember a group of us getting together at the hospital praying. I paced back and forth inside and outside of the ER. I remember my sister was around the corner and I looked into her eyes and it didn't make me feel any better. I knew it wasn't good. I remember this man wanting to see me so I walked back inside and not realizing who he introduced himself as, but I kept listening to what he was saying.

He told me he was the chaplain and he was here for support and the doctors will be talking with me shortly. I then went into a room waiting to talk with the doctor. My pastor at the time accompanied me. **The doctor came in and introduced himself and began to tell me that he got shot in the neck a few times and how the bullets went down in his body piercing organs. He told me he had to open him to pump his heart being that he lost him but he started back breathing. He started telling me things he was doing to him, then stated again, that he had to pump his heart a second time but that this time it was unsuccessful and he couldn't bring him back. All I heard was bring him back over and over in**

my head. I began to scream out saying, "my son is dead, oh God not Josh." I wanted to see Josh but the doctor had told me that I couldn't, being that he was still on the surgery table with his body cut open and I wouldn't want to see him like that.

Still in disbelief that this couldn't be real, a feeling that's not a feeling, a numbness went all over my body. Leaving the hospital all I remember was seeing a lot of people. I was leaving the hospital without my son and they said he was dead. I was crushed, "how could this be, Lord? My baby, my oldest son is gone, my Josh is gone." I went home and finally fell asleep only to wake up to realize it was real, I wasn't dreaming, this horrendous event actually did happen. I realized that last night I didn't get my call from him nor did I get one from him this morning. I didn't hear his voice. I couldn't call him and when I did call his number he didn't answer. **"So, this is real, I will never hear my son's voice again, I never will hear him call me "Ma", I will never hear him say "you feel me…"** "Why Lord? What do I do now? You said that you wouldn't put more on me than I could bare! Lord tell me how do I bare the loss of my son? Tell me how that hole in my heart, that missing piece is going to mend back together? Tell me how to handle a piece of me that is gone forever? Tell me how do I bury my son, that's supposed to bury me? Oh my God, I trust You and need You to come see about me", these were the painful words coming out of my mouth.

Days later while I was at the store picking out a suit for my son to be buried in, tears started flowing, still in disbelief that what happened was real, the thought of "my son being actually murdered and gone from me forever", was an overwhelming feeling that I wouldn't wish on any mother or father or parental figure. The day of the viewing of his body, all I could do is stare at him in the casket. He still looked the same, just a little darker, but that was my 20-year-old son laying cold, dead and stiff in a casket. I started asking God again how I could handle this when the next day was his funeral. I began to feel the Lord's presence and it felt like it overshadowed me. I began to think about his last month and the last two weeks of his life and how the Lord knew this day was going to happen. I thought about how the Lord loved me enough to allow me to experience and see the change in my son; how the Lord loved me enough to allow me to get my last hug and my last verbal "I love you" from Josh 2 hours before he got shot; how the Lord led him his last day alive to be spent with me in church; I thought about his last words to me before leaving the church, "I'm Happy". All this gave me the strength that I needed for the day of his burial. God allowed my son enough time to make it right with Him and people. I thought about the topic Josh talked about in my living room "You can run but You can't hide..." The Lord constantly gave me that supernatural strength daily and without Him I would not have been able to endure the loss of my eldest son.

These sobering stories are all real! They are friends of mine that I personally know and knew. You see, while you may look at my story and say to yourself, "Oh, he did all that he did and he made it back, I can do the same",

understand this, everybody doesn't make it back with their life or with their freedom!

Chapter Nineteen

Past, Present & Future

I hope that you, the reader of this book has learned some very important things! The purpose of me writing this, was not to glorify anything that I have done. What's done is done! My hope and prayer is that you take time to evaluate your own life and come to the conclusion that I have, that, ***serving the Lord is the best thing on earth!***

In this last chapter, I will highlight some of my feelings along with things that I am presently doing, where I am headed with the goals that I have, and what I have learned through the process of my life thus far.

Feelings

There is no way that I could chronicle all that I have done. I have merely taken a few incidences and stories and placed them in this book. You often hear people say that they wouldn't change the things that they have done because it has made them who they are. My truth in regards to that statement is that I would change the majority of what I have done, because it would've still made me into a person just with different stories. I'm ok with that.

I have eight biological children by five different women and one bonus daughter with my wife. I am happy to have all of these children, and while I have nine, there are so many people in the world that are not able to have any children.

One of the biggest challenges is that these children live in different states, some with me and some with their mothers but none of them are able to get the full-on balanced life of living together with their birth mothers and birth father nor are they able to grow up with each other as siblings. This pains me every day!

In addition, I have trust issues when it comes to people because of all of the people I have stolen from or robbed, and/or things that have been taken from me, which causes me to live with a feeling that someone is always trying to do something slick and sly behind my back, versus outright trusting people that I should naturally trust.

I've committed numerous crimes, carried several guns, hurt a lot of people, and broken a lot of women's hearts by my manipulating ways. I've done so many things in my life, in such a short amount of time and it hurts me internally knowing that I have wronged people, which though I am forgiven by God, I have not forgotten.

This is What I'm Doing

In spite of all that I have done, God has redeemed me and brought me a long way! I graduated from Oakwood University in 2016 with a Bachelor's Degree (BA) in Ministerial Theology. I graduated with my Masters of Divinity (M.Div) Degree from Andrews Universities Theological Seminary in 2018. A few months before I graduated from Oakwood University, I was hired by the Northeastern Conference (NEC) of Seventh-day Adventist to pastor. I was with NEC from 2016-2023. From January 2024-July 2024, I pastored with Lake Region Conference (LRC). I completed my doctoral degree in 2023 also from Andrews University having a Doctorate in Ministry (D.Min) in the Intergenerational Church. I have completed a couple of units of Clinical Pastoral Education (CPE), and currently live in Philadelphia, PA as my wife and I build a ministry to bridge the gap between the Church and the community.

This is Where I'm Headed

I intend to write more books, having published two now. This one, and another entitled, "A Trail of Tears: Strength for the Challenges We Face Transitioning from the Streets to Society", which is written to help people transition while in prison and out of prison.

Lastly, my wife and I will continue to build the ministry fulfilling whatever the Lord calls us to and wherever He calls us to go.

This is What I Have Learned

The Bible is very interesting to me. In it, are very real stories of people like you and I who had the same struggles as each of us do. One in particular stands out; his name is King Solomon. This Biblical figure is responsible for writing three books in the Old Testament of the Bible. These books include: Proverbs, Song of Solomon and Ecclesiastes.

Solomon is known for several things, but one of the main things that interest me, as it relates to what I have learned throughout my life, is something that he wrote in the book of Ecclesiastes. He states in Chapter 12 Verses 1, 13 and 14, quoting from the ESV Bible version, ***"Remember also your Creator in the days of your youth, before the evil days come and the years draw near…The end of the matter; all has been heard. Fear (Worship) God and keep his commandments, for this is the whole duty of man. For God will bring every deed into judgment, with every secret thing, whether good or evil."***

When you understand the fact that Solomon is speaking these things after having hundreds of women, all the money one could ever want, all the power in the world and anything else you could imagine, it brings what he is saying in these texts quoted above more into focus.

For me, I did not have all of what King Solomon had, however, I did a lot of things in my years running from God, some of which you have read in the chapters above.

In hindsight I've realized through all of what I have done, that the best thing in the world is to worship the God of heaven and earth! I cannot speak for anyone else in this world, but speaking for myself, building my personal relationship with God and serving Him has been the greatest experience! But it's up to you to experience Him for yourself.

Final Words

I hope that this book has been more than mere fun and exhilarating stories. My hope and prayer is that you take what you have read, seeing the many things that I have done and seeing the results of some of my friends listed, that you yourself will make better decisions then we did. It's your decision to make, but my prayer for you is that you, reading this book, make the best decision of all, and choose God!

JailLyfe: Jesus Always Is Looking
Love Your Friends & Your Enemies

Chapter Twenty

Pictures of the Past and Present

My brother Adam and I (1998)

Celebrating Pastoring (2019)

Knitted Blanket by Brandon Bernard

(2017)

Family Photo (1994)

Pastoring (2019)

Myself (2005)

Holliday Transfer Unit (2001)

My brother Adam and I (1998)

Myself, Mom and Brother (1983)

Doctoral Class (2019)

Andrews University Student (2018)

Myself, Mom and Brother (1982)

Myself and Daughter Shynik (2004)

Some of my kids: Andrew, Simone,

Summer, Shynik, Aaron aka Tato (2019)

Myself with tattoo on my face and hair in two ponytails (2005)

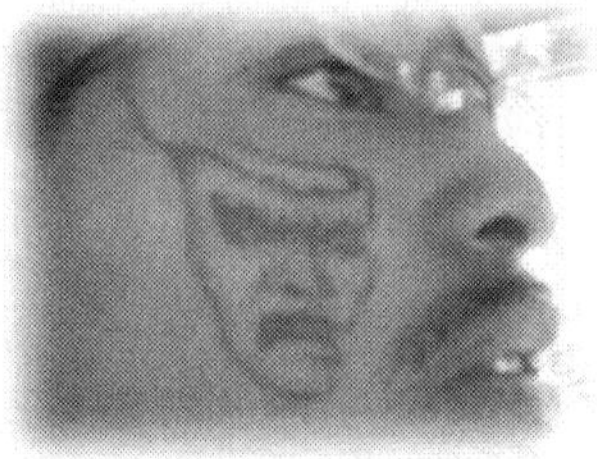

First session to get tattoo off my face (2010)

Brother, Myself and Cousin Roger (2018)

Daughter Caysen and Myself (2018)

Myself and Dr. Case, my main professor during doctoral course, Mock Graduation (2019)

Myself in Eagles Gear (2020)

My Brother and Father (2023)

Daughter Caysen and I (2022)

Father's Gravesite (2024)

Kids and I: Nehemiah, Tato, Myself,

Andrew and Shynik (2023)

Myself (1997/98)

My graduation from Oakwood University:

Myself and Brother (2016)

Mother and Father (2023)

Mother and Father (2023)

Super Bowl: Brother and I (2023)

Super Bowl: Brother and I (2023)

Super Bowl: Brother and I (2023)

Super Bowl: Brother and I (2023)

Myself and Daughter Zemora (2024)

Myself and Wife Shackarah (2024)

My wife and I (2024)

Son: Xavier (2022)

Son: Xavier (2022)

Terre Haute Federal Prison: Brandon

Bernard (2016)

Federal Prison: Brandon Bernard (2017)

Federal Prison: Brandon and I (2020)

Brandon's Gravesite (2022)

Brandon Bernard Newspaper Clip the Day

after His Execution (2020)

Josh (2012)

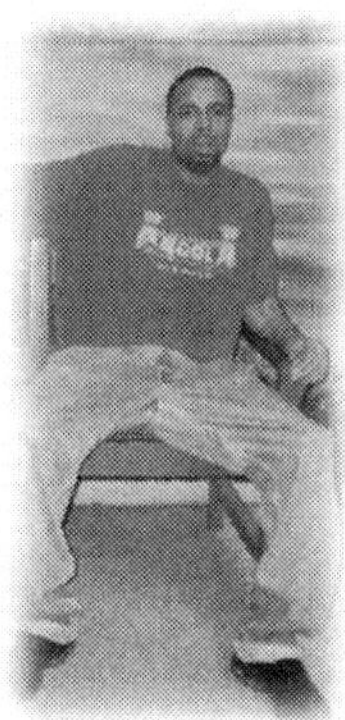

Prescott: Angola State Prison (2011)

Prison Bootcamp: Myself (1999)

Prison ID: Myself (2002)

Doctoral Class (2022)

THE END

Made in the USA
Middletown, DE
27 January 2025